A SHI'ITE ANTHOLOGY

A SHI'ITE ANTHOLOGY

Selected and with a Foreword by
ᶜAllāmah Sayyid Muḥammad Ḥusayn Ṭabāṭabā'ī
Translated with Explanatory Notes by
William C. Chittick
Under the Direction of and with an Introduction by
Seyyed Hossein Nasr

State University of New York Press Albany

MUHAMMADI TRUST OF GREAT BRITAIN & NORTHERN IRELAND
London

First published 1980 by Muhammadi Trust of Great Britain and Northern Ireland.

For information, address State University of New York
Press, State University Plaza, Albany, N.Y., 12246

ISBN, 87395-510-2
87395-511-0 (pbk.)

10 9 8 7 6 5 4 3 2

TRANSLITERATION

Arabic Letter	Transliteration
ء	ʼ
ب	b
ت	t
ث	th
ج	j
ح	ḥ
خ	kh
د	d
ذ	dh
ر	r
ز	z
س	s
ش	sh
ص	ṣ
ض	ḍ
ط	ṭ
ظ	ẓ
ع	ʻ
غ	gh
ف	f
ق	q
ك	k
ل	l
م	m
ن	n
ه	h
و	w
ي	y
ة	t

Short Vowels

ـَ	a
ـُ	u
ـِ	i

Long Vowels

ـَا	ā
ـُو	ū
ـِي	ī

Diphthongs

ـَوْ	aw
ـَيْ	ay
ـِيّ	iyy
ـُوّ	uww

Persian Letters

پ	p
چ	ch
ژ	zh
گ	g

ACKNOWLEDGMENT

The Muhammadi Trust wishes to express its gratitude to its patrons for their willing and kind support to make this publication possible.

CONTENTS

IN THE NAME OF ALLAH MOST MERCIFUL
AND COMPASSIONATE

INTRODUCTION

Despite the vast amount of scholarship carried out by Western orientalists since the nineteenth century and the analyses and translations made of various Islamic sources, very little attention has been paid thus far to the collection of religious sayings, sermons, prayers, proverbs and didactic expositions which comprises the corpus of *Ḥadīth* as understood by Twelve-Imam Shi'ite Muslims. It is of course true that much of the substance of the Shi'ite *ḥadīth* collection resembles the Sunni collection,[1] and to the extent that the latter has been studied the former has also been dealt with in an indirect manner. But inasmuch as Shi'ite *ḥadīths* possess a form, style and "perfume" of their own, no indirect treatment of their substance and content can replace the direct translation and analysis of this collection itself.

It is in fact rather amazing that despite the extreme importance of Shi'ite *Ḥadīth* for the development of Shi'ite law and theology as well as many fields of the "intellectual sciences" (*al-ᶜulūm al-ᶜaqliyyah*), not to speak of its role in piety and the spiritual life, the sayings of the Imams of Shi'ism have not been rendered into English until now. Nor have they been studied as a whole and as a distinct body of religious writings of an inspired nature within the general context of Islam itself. The present volume represents, therefore, a pioneering effort to present a sample of this extensive body of writings to the English speaking world.

The Shi'ite *ḥadīth* literature includes all the sayings of the Prophet of Islam accepted by Shi'ites as well as the traditions of the twelve Imams from ᶜAlī ibn Abī Ṭālib to the Mahdī. This collection is thus considered to be, after the Holy Quran, the most important body of religious texts for Shi'ites. As in Sunni Islam, so in this case: the *Ḥadīth* forms along with the Revealed Book the basis of all the religious sciences, including of course the

Sharīah as well as religious life in both its intellectual and devotional aspects. No aspect of the life and history of the Shi'ite community would be comprehensible without a consideration of this body of inspired writings.

What is particular to this collection, however, is that although it is a part of the foundation of Islam as seen by Shi'ism, its "composition" stretches over a period of more than two centuries. In Sunni Islam, *Ḥadīth* is limited to the sayings of the Blessed Prophet. In fact to use the term "*ḥadīth*" in Sunnism is to refer to *his* sayings and not to anyone else's. In the case of Shi'ism, however, although a clear distinction is made between prophetic *Ḥadīth* (*al-ḥadīth al-nabawī*) and the sayings of the Imams (*al-ḥadīth al-walawī*), the two are included in a single collection. This means that from a certain point of view the apostolic age of Islam is seen by Shi'ism to stretch way beyond the relatively short period usually associated with apostles in various religions.

The reason for this perspective lies of course in the Shi'ite conception of the Imam.[2] The term *imām* as used in a technical sense in Shi'ism differs from the general usage of the term in Arabic, where it means "leader", or in Sunni political theory where it means the caliph himself. As used technically in Shi'ism the term refers to the person who contains within himself the "Muhammadan Light" (*al-nūr al-muḥammadī*) which was handed down through Fāṭimah, the daughter of the Blessed Prophet, and ᶜAlī, the first Imam, to the others, terminating with the Hidden Imam who is to appear again one day as the Mahdī.[3] As a result of the presence of this light, the Imam is considered to be "sinless" (*maᶜṣūm*) and to possess perfect knowledge of the esoteric as well as the exoteric order.

The Imams are like a chain of light issuing forth from the "Sun of Prophecy" which is their origin, and yet they are never separated from that Sun. Whatever is said by them emanates from the same inviolable treasury of inspired wisdom. Since they are an extension of the inner reality of the Blessed Prophet, their words really go back to him. That is why their sayings are seen in the Shi'ite perspective as an extension of the prophetic *Ḥadīth*, just as the light of their being is seen as a continuation of the prophetic light. In Shi'ite eyes, the temporal separation of the Imams from the Blessed Prophet does not at all affect their essential and inner bond with him or the continuity of the "prophetic light" which is the source of his as well as their inspired knowledge.

This metaphysical conception is the reason that Shiʿites incorporate traditions stretching over two centuries into a single whole with those of the Blessed Prophet himself. It also distinguishes the Shiʿite conception of *Ḥadīth* from that held in Sunnism. Otherwise, the actual content of *Ḥadīth* in Sunni and Shiʿite collections is very close. After all, both kinds concern the same spiritual reality. Of course the chain of transmission accepted by the two schools is not the same. But despite this difference in the authorities who have handed down the prophetic sayings, the actual *ḥadīths* recorded by Sunni and Shiʿite sources have overwhelming similarities. The major difference is the Shiʿites' consideration of the extension of an aspect of the being of the Blessed Prophet in the Imams and therefore their addition of the sayings of the Imams to the strictly "prophetic" *Ḥadīth.*

The sayings of the Imams are in many ways not only a continuation but also a kind of commentary and elucidation of the prophetic *Ḥadīth*, often with the aim of bringing out the esoteric teachings of Islam. Many of these *ḥadīths* deal, like those of the Blessed Prophet, with the practical aspects of life and the *Sharīʿah.* Others deal with pure metaphysics, as do certain prophetic *ḥadīths*, especially the "sacred *ḥadīths*" (*ḥadīth qudsī*). Still other sayings of the Imams deal with the devotional aspects of life and contain some of the most famous prayers which have been recited over the ages by both Sunnis and Shiʿites. Finally some of the sayings deal with the various esoteric sciences. They thus cover a vast spectrum ranging from the "mundane" problems of daily life to the question of the meaning of truth itself. Because of their innate nature and also the fact that like Sufism they issue from the esoteric dimension of Islam, they have intermingled over the ages with certain types of Sufi writings.[4] They have also been considered as sources of Islamic esotericism by the Sufis, because the Imams of Shiʿism are seen in the Sufi perspective as the spiritual poles of their age. They appear in the spiritual chain (*silsilah*) of various Sufi orders, even those which have spread almost exclusively among Sunnis.[5]

Because of the nature of their contents, these sayings have influenced nearly every branch of Shiʿite learning as well as the daily life of the community. Shiʿite jurisprudence (*fiqh*) bases itself directly upon this corpus in addition to the Holy Quran.

Shi'ite theology (*kalām*) would be incomprehensible without a knowledge of these sayings. Shi'ite Quranic commentaries draw heavily upon them. Even sciences of nature such as natural history or alchemy were developed with reference to them. And finally these sayings have surfaced as sources for meditation of the most sublime metaphysical themes over the centuries, and some of the most elaborate metaphysical and philosophical schools of Islam have issued to a large extent from them. Later Islamic philosophy as associated with the name of Ṣadr al-Dīn Shīrāzī, would in fact be inconceivable without recourse to the Shi'ite *ḥadīth* collection.[6] One of Ṣadr al-Dīn's greatest metaphysical works is his unfinished commentary upon a portion of the most important of the four basic Shi'ite collections of *Ḥadīth*, the *al-Kāfī* of al-Kulaynī.[7]

Within the collection of Shi'ite *ḥadīths* are certain works which need to be mentioned separately. There is first of all the celebrated *Nahj al-balāghah* (*The Path of Eloquence*) of ᶜAlī ibn Abī Ṭālib assembled and systematized by the fourth/tenth century Shi'ite scholar Sayyid Sharīf al-Raḍī. Considering the enormous importance of this work in Shi'ite Islam as well as for all lovers of the Arabic language, it is remarkable how little attention has been paid to it in European languages.[8] After all, many of the leading writers of Arabic such as Ṭāhā Ḥusayn and Kurd ᶜAlī claim in their autobiographies to have perfected their style of writing Arabic through the study of the *Nahj al-balāghah*, while generation after generation of Shi'ite thinkers have meditated and commented upon its meaning. Moreover, the shorter prayers and proverbs of this work have spread very widely among the populace and have entered both the classical and folk literature of not only Arabic but also Persian, and through the influence of Persian, several other languages of the Islamic peoples, such as Urdu.

The *Nahj al-balāghah* contains, besides spiritual advice, moral maxims and political directives, several remarkable discourses on metaphysics, especially concerning the question of Unity (*al-tawḥīd*). It possesses both its own method of exposition and a very distinct technical vocabulary which distinguish it from the various Islamic schools which have dealt with metaphysics.

Western scholars refused for a long time to accept the authenticity of the authorship of this work and attributed it to Sayyid Sharīf al-Raḍī, although the style of al-Raḍī's own works is very different from that of the *Nahj al-balāghah*. In any case as far as the traditional Shi'ite perspective is concerned, the position of the *Nahj al-balāghah* and its authorship can best be explained by repeating a conversation which took place some eighteen or nineteen years ago between ᶜAllāmah Ṭabāṭabā'ī, the celebrated contemporary Shi'ite scholar who is responsible for the selection of the present anthology, and Henry Corbin, the foremost Western student of Shi'ism. Corbin, who himself was as far removed from "historicism" as possible, once said to ᶜAllāmah Ṭabāṭabā'ī during the regular discussions they had together in Tehran (in which the present writer usually acted as translator), "Western scholars claim that ᶜAlī is not the author of the *Nahj al-balāghah.* What is your view and whom do you consider to be the author of this work?" ᶜAllāmah Ṭabāṭabā'ī raised his head and answered in his usual gentle and calm manner, "For us whoever wrote the *Nahj al-balāghah is* ᶜAlī, even if he lived a century ago."

The second notable work in the Shi'ite collection of *Ḥadīth* is the *al-Ṣaḥīfat al-sajjādiyyah* (*The Scroll of al-Sajjād*) of the fourth Imam Zayn al-ᶜĀbidīn, also called al-Sajjād. A witness to the tragedy of Karbala — which must have left an indelible impression upon his soul — the fourth Imam poured forth his inner life in a symphony of beautiful prayers which have caused the *Ṣaḥīfah* to be called the "Psalms of the Family of the Holy Prophet". These prayers form a part of the daily religious life of not only Shi'ites but also Sunnis, who find them in many of the prayer manuals most popular in the Sunni world[9].

Also notable in the Shi'ite collection of *Ḥadīth* are the sayings of the fifth, sixth and seventh Imams, from whom the largest number of traditions have been recorded. These Imams lived at the end of the Umayyad and beginning of the Abbasid dynasties when, as a result of the changes in the caliphate, central authority had weakened and the Imams were able to speak more openly and also train more students. The number of students, both Shi'ite and Sunni, trained by the sixth Imam Jaᶜfar al-Ṣādiq has been estimated at four thousand. He left behind a vast body of sayings which range from the field of law to the esoteric sciences.

The sayings of the Holy Prophet and the Imams have been of course a constant source of meditation and discussion by Shi'ite men of learning throughout the ages. But it is especially in the later period of Shi'ite history beginning with Sayyid Ḥaydar Āmulī, leading to the great masters of the Safavid period such as

Mīr Dāmād and Mullā Ṣadrā and continuing to the present day that these sayings have served as a distinct source for metaphysics and philosophy as well as the juridical and Quranic sciences. The commentaries of Mullā Ṣadrā, Qāḍī Saᶜīd al-Qummī and many others on these collections of Shiʿite *Ḥadīth* are among the great masterpieces of Islamic thought.[10] Later Islamic philosophy and theosophy in fact could not be understood without them.[11]

The present volume represents the second in a series of three which was planned many years ago with the help and support of Professor Kenneth Morgan, then of Colgate University, with the aim of presenting Shiʿism to the Western world from the point of view of Shiʿism itself. The first volume in the series appeared in English as *Shiʿite Islam* by ᶜAllāmah Sayyid Muḥammad Ḥusayn Ṭabāṭabāʾī, edited and translated by the author of these lines.[12] The second volume, called *The Quran in Islam* (*Qurʾān dar islām*), was also written by ᶜAllāmah Ṭabāṭabāʾī and its Persian version printed in Tehran. Most of it was also translated by us into English, but the translation was not completed. The events of the last year in Iran have made the manuscript of what we have already translated inaccessible to us so that there is no possibility at the present moment to produce the English translation as planned.

The present volume is the third and final one in the series. After a long period of study and deliberation, ᶜAllāmah Ṭabāṭabāʾī made the present selection from the vast collection of *Ḥadīth*, a task which would have been bewildering for anyone not possessing his knowledge of this inspired literature. Once this selection was made, Dr. William Chittick, who was then residing in Tehran and working with us on various scholarly projects, undertook the arduous task of translating the very compact and difficult Arabic texts into English. Because of the lack of precedence for rendering these writings into European languages and the nature of the texts themselves, Dr. Chittick was faced with a formidable task. It was only his intimate knowledge of Arabic, Persian and the subject matter combined with great patience and meticulous scholarship that made it possible for him to succeed in such a laborious and exacting undertaking. He should be congratulated in every way for having successfully concluded this colossal task.

It remained for the Muhammadi Trust to bring the project to fruition and to make its publication possible. The credit for this volume and its effect in making Shiʿism better known must be given to a large extent to the Trust. As one who was responsible for this volume from its inception, I want to thank the Trust especially Wg. Cdr. (ret'd.) Q. Husayn, its very able secretary who with great love and devotion to the true cause of Islam, enabled us to complete this project. Dr. Chittick, also, has earned the gratitude of all students of Islam for his fine scholarship and devotion to the completion of a very difficult project.

This volume is particularly pertinent at the present moment, when volcanic eruptions and powerful waves of a political nature associated with the name of Islam in general and Shi'ism in particular have made an authentic knowledge of things Islamic imperative, lest ignorance destroy the very foundations of human society and the relations which make discourse between various nations and religious communities possible.

At the dawn of this fifteenth century of the terrestrial existence of Islam, may this volume be an aid in bringing about an understanding of one of the fundamental sources of inspiration and knowledge for not only Shi'ism but Islam as such.

wa'Llāhu a'lam

Seyyed Hossein Nasr
Cambridge, Massachusetts
Muḥarram 1400
November 1979

NOTES

1 There are six canonical collections in Sunni Islam which have been accepted by the whole community since they were first compiled in the second and third Islamic centuries. These collections, referred to as *al-Ṣiḥāḥ al-sittah*, the *Six Correct Collections*, are associated with the names of great scholars of *Ḥadīth* such as Bukhārī, Muslim, etc. Of these, the most famous is that of Bukhārī, which has fortunately been translated into English (*Ṣaḥīḥ al-Bukhārī: Arabic-English*, by Muhammad Muhsin Khan, Islamic University, Madina; second revised edition, Ankara, 1976). The vast concordance of *Ḥadīth* by Wensinck, Mensing et al. (Leiden, 1936-69) is based on these six collections.

2 See ᶜAllāmah Ṭabāṭabā'ī, *Shi'ite Islam*, London-Albany, 1975, pp. 173ff.

3 As far as the continuity of the chain is concerned the Ismāᶜīlī conception is of course different, since for the Ismāᶜīlīs the chain of Imams continues uninterrupted to this day.

4 On the relation between Shi'ism and Sufism see S. H. Nasr, *Sufi Essays*, London, 1972, pp. 104-20.

5 A most interesting example of such interpenetration is to be seen in part of the famous prayer of the third Shi'ite Imam Ḥusayn, also found in Shādhilī prayer manuals. See W. Chittick, "A Shādhilī Presence in Shi'ite Islam", *Sophia Perennis*, vol. I, no. 1, 1975, pp. 97-100.

6 On this corpus as a source for the doctrines of Ṣadr al-Dīn Shīrāzī see S. H. Nasr, *Ṣadr al-Dīn Shīrāzī and His Transcendent Theosophy*, London-Boulder, 1978, chapter 4.

7 This monumental work was translated into French by H. Corbin, who taught it for many years in Paris, but it has never been published. See Corbin, *En Islam iranien*, Paris, 1971.

8 This work has been translated several times in part or wholly in the Indo-Pakistani sub-continent and in Iran, but none of these translations is completely adequate. A new translation has been prepared by S. H. Jafri which is supposed to be published soon and which, we hope, will fulfill the very difficult condition of doing justice to both the meaning and the literary beauty of the text.

9 Some of these prayers have been translated by C. Padwick in her *Muslim Devotions*, London, 1961.

10 See H. Corbin, *En Islam iranien.*

11 Not only Mullā Ṣadrā, but also his students were deeply influenced by this collection. One of Mullā Ṣadrā's most famous students, Mullā Muḥsin Fayḍ Kāshānī, who was at once theologian, gnostic and philosopher, was also

an outstanding authority on Shi'ite *Ḥadīth*. His *al-Wāfī* is one of the most often studied works on the *ḥadīths* of the Shi'ite Imams and their lines of transmission.
12 In our introduction to that work we have dealt with the conditions under which these works were conceived as well as a biography of ʿAllāmah Ṭabāṭabā'ī. *Shi'ite Islam* was published by both Allen & Unwin in London and the State University of New York Press in Albany. The work has also just appeared in paperback in America. It is of interest to note that the original Persian version of this work, written specifically for this project and with a Persian introduction by S. H. Nasr, has become one of the most widely read works on Shi'ism in Iran itself and has been reprinted many times.

TRANSLATOR'S INTRODUCTION

In works on Islam the word "*ḥadīth*" usually refers to the sayings or "traditions" which have been transmitted from the Prophet. Muslims hold these to be the most important source of Islamic teachings after the Qur'ān. Numerous works have been written in Western languages on the role of the *ḥadīth* literature in Islam[1] and a number of important translations have been made.[2] But almost all Western studies have been limited to the point of view of Sunni Islam and based on Sunni sources and collections. Practically no one has paid any serious attention to the different nature of the *ḥadīth* literature in Shi'ism and the different sources from which the *ḥadīths* are derived.

The fundamental distinction to be made between Shi'ite and Sunni *ḥadīths* is that in Shi'ism the traditions are not limited to those of the Prophet, but include those of the Imams as well. As important and basic as this point is, it has not been understood even in such standard reference works as the new *Encyclopaedia of Islam*. There the author of the article "*Ḥadīth*" is aware that there is some difference between Shi'ism and Sunnism on the question of which *ḥadīths* are included, but he thinks that it lies in the fact that the Shi'ite collections accept "only traditions traced through ᶜAlī's family." But this is incorrect, since numerous traditions are also transmitted through other sources. What the author fails to mention is that the *ḥadīth* literature as understood by Shi'ites is not limited to the sayings of the Prophet, but includes those of the Imams as well.[3]

In short, collections of *ḥadīths* in Sunni Islam, such as those of al-Bukhārī and Muslim, contain only sayings transmitted from and about the Prophet. But the Shi'ite collections, such as that of al-Kulaynī, also contain sayings transmitted from and about the twelve Imams. Naturally the Shi'ites make a distinction among the *ḥadīths*, so that those transmitted from the Prophet are of greater authority, but nevertheless all traditions are listed together according to subject matter, not according to author.

The most famous and authoritative collections of Shi'ite *ḥadīths* are four works which, in terms of their importance for Shi'ism, correspond to the *Six Correct Collections* in Sunni Islam. These are *al-Kāfī fī ᶜilm al-dīn* (*The Sufficient in the Knowledge of Religion*) by Thiqat al-Islām Muḥammad ibn Yaᶜqūb al-Kulaynī (d. 329/940), *Man lā yaḥḍuruhu al-faqīh* (*For him not in the Presence of a Jurisprudent*) of Shaykh al-Ṣadūq Muḥammad ibn Bābūyah al-Qummī (d. 381/991), *Tahdhīb al-aḥkām* (*Rectification of the Statutes*) by Shaykh al-Ṭā'ifah Muḥammad al-Ṭūsī (d. 460/1068) and *al-Istibṣār fī mā ukhtulif fīhi min al-akhbār* (*Reflection upon the Disputed Traditions*) also by al-Ṭūsī.

The Present Collection

The sermons, sayings, prayers and writings translated here present a cross section of Shi'ite religious thought with an emphasis upon that which is most basic for the religion itself and most universal and hence understandable in the eyes of non-Muslims. As ᶜAllāmah Ṭabāṭabā'ī points out in his foreword, in making these selections his aim was to emphasize the three basic dimensions of the Shi'ite tradition: 1. The profession of Unity (*al-tawḥīd*), or the metaphysical and theological principles of the faith. 2. The political, social and moral teachings. 3. The inward, spiritual and devotional life of the community. Hence the selections stress the principles and fundamentals (*uṣūl*) of Islam, while they tend to ignore the branches and secondary aspects (*furūᶜ*). In other words, little is said about the concrete ramifications of the principles in terms of the details of the application of the Divine Law (*al-Sharīᶜah*) to everyday life. Nevertheless, the secondary aspects are clearly reflected in ᶜAlī's "Instructions to Mālik al-Ashtar" and to a lesser degree in the prayers.

Although it is well known that the first "pillar of Islam" is the profession of faith, which begins with a statement of the Divine Unity, Western scholars have tended to explain the Islamic belief in God's Oneness as a relatively simple-minded affirmation of the existence of only one God. Perhaps one reason the *Nahj al-balāghah* and the Shi'ite *ḥadīth* literature in general have been neglected or simply branded as spurious is that their very existence flatly contradicts the commonly accepted idea of a simple bedouin faith with few philosophical or metaphysical overtones. In these writings we see that already in the first centuries of Islam the Divine Unity was affirmed in terms reminiscent of the subtlety of later "theosophical" Sufism, but still completely steeped in the peculiar spiritual aroma of the revelation itself.

The Sources

In making the selections ᶜAllāmah Ṭabāṭabā'ī utilized four works: the *Nahj al-balāghah*, *al-Ṣaḥīfat al-sajjādiyyah*, *Biḥār al-anwār* and *Mafātīḥ al-jinān*. The first two works are discussed in Dr. Nasr's introduction. *Biḥār al-anwār* (*Oceans of Lights*) is a monumental encyclopaedia of *ḥadīths* which attempts to collect all Sh'ite traditions in a single work and which classifies them by subject matter. It was compiled in the Safavid period by the famous theologian Muḥammad Bāqir Majlisī (d. 1110/1698-9 or 1111/1699-1700). The importance the work has possessed since its compilation as the standard reference work for all Shi'ite studies can hardly be overemphasized. One indication of its popularity is that, despite its enormous size, it was published twice in lithographed form in the nineteenth century. The modern edition of the work fills 110 volumes of approximately 400 pages each.

Majlisī collected his traditions from numerous earlier sources. As examples, we can mention a few of the works from which he derived the *ḥadīths* in the present collection, works which have been independently published in modern times. Shaykh al-Ṣadūq, the author of one of the four basic works on Shi'ite *ḥadīths* referred to above, compiled dozens of authoritative *ḥadīth* collections, each of which usually follows a particular theme. His *al-Tawḥīd* collects traditions which illustrate the profession of God's Unity. His *ᶜUyūn akhbār al-Riḍā* gathers together everything that has been related about Imam ᶜAlī al-Riḍā, the eighth Imam, whose tomb in Mashhad is the holiest site of pilgrimage in Iran. The work contains such things as descriptions of the Imam's mother, explanations of the reason his name was chosen, all the sayings which have been recorded from him, and traditions concerning his death and the miracles which have occurred at his tomb. Shaykh al-Ṣadūq's *al-Khiṣāl* demonstrates the importance of numbers in the traditions. In twelve long chapters he records all the *ḥadīths* which mention the numbers one to twelve. The author of *al-Iḥtijāj*, Abū Manṣūr Aḥmad ibn ᶜAlī al-Ṭabarsī (d. 599/1202-3), rejects the views of certain of his contemporaries who had claimed that the Prophet and the Imams never engaged in argumentation. He collects together traditions in which their discussions with opponents have been recorded.

The fourth work from which ᶜAllāmah Ṭabāṭabā'ī made his selections is *Mafātīḥ al-jinān* ("Keys to the Gardens of Paradise"), a standard collection of Shi'ite prayers compiled from *Biḥār al-anwār* and other sources by ᶜAbbās Qummī (d. 1359/1940-1). It includes prayers to be recited daily, prayers for special occasions such as religious holidays and days of mourning, litanies and invocations for different moments in one's life, instructions for making a pilgrimage to the tomb of the Prophet or any one of the Imams, and prayers for every other conceivable occasion as well.

The Translations

A note needs to be added about the method of translation. Because of the sacred nature of the texts and their fundamental importance as sources for the Shi'ite branch of Islam, I have attempted to translate them in a strictly literal manner so that the least amount of personal interpretation will have been made. There are definite disadvantages to this method, but the necessity for an accurate translation would seem to outweigh them all. After all, the Quran has been translated dozens of times. Others who may feel that the present translation does not do justice to the literary qualities of the text may try their own hand at rendering it into English.

The necessity for a literal translation is all the greater because a good deal of the material translated here — in particular those parts which derive from the *Nahj al-balāghah* — has also been translated elsewhere and on the whole has been misrepresented. Before such interpretive translations are made and held to reflect the thought of the Imams, literal translations are of paramount importance. In order to maintain a faithful translation, I have added notes wherever I deviate from a strictly literal translation or wherever there are questionable readings in the original.

Because no standard translations exist for many technical terms,

I have felt it necessary to add the Arabic original in brackets for the benefit of scholars and Arabic speakers. This is especially true in the most difficult and metaphysical section of the book, Part I "On the Unity of God." Although the Arabic terms will prove a distraction to most readers, they represent the only practical way of tying the present texts into the reader's knowledge of the Arabic language.

Finally I would like to express my sincere gratitude to Seyyed Hossein Nasr, who asked me to undertake this work many years ago and has guided me in every stage of it, although of course I remain completely responsible for any inaccuracies which may remain in the translations and notes. Peter Lamborn Wilson and William Shpall also read the manuscript and made valuable suggestions. And without the kindness and encouragement of Wg. Cdr. (rtd.) Husayn and the Muhammadi Trust, the work may never have been completed and published.

NOTES

1 On the subject of prophetic *Ḥadīth* in general see the article "*Ḥadīth*" in the *Encyclopaedia of Islam* (new edition), where a good bibliography is also provided (vol. III, pp. 23-8).

2 Perhaps the most important *ḥadīth* collection yet to be completely translated into worthy English is the *Mishkāt al-maṣābīḥ*, trans. by J. Robson, Lahore, 4 vols., 1963-5. See also the translation of Bukhārī mentioned in note 1 of the introduction, and *Ṣaḥīḥ Muslim*, trans. by A. K. Ṣiddīqī, Lahore, 1972 onward.

3 *The Encyclopaedia of Islam*, vol. III, p. 24.

FOREWORD

If one studies the literature of Islam carefully, one will immediately encounter a vast and varied field of material. First there is the network of laws and regulations which makes up Islamic jurisprudence (*fiqh*) and which takes into consideration and regulates man's every individual and social "movement and rest", activity and situation, at every moment of time, in every place and under all conditions, as well as every particular and general occurrence related to human life. Second there is a vast range of moral and ethical expositions which weighs every sort of moral activity, whether praiseworthy or blamable, and presents as a model for human society that which befits the perfection of man. Finally on the level of Islam's overall view of Reality there is the general "philosophy" of Islam, that is, its sciences relating to cosmology, spiritual anthropology and finally the knowledge of God, presented in the clearest possible expression and most direct manner.

On a more profound level of study and penetration it will become obvious that the various elements of this tradition, with all their astonishing complexity and variety, are governed by a particular kind of interrelationship; that all of these elements are reducible in the final analysis to one truth, the "Profession of God's Unity" (*tawḥīd*), which is the ultimate principle of all the Islamic sciences. "A good word is as a good tree — its roots are in heaven, it gives its produce every season by the leave of its Lord" (Quran XIV, 24).

The noble sayings and writings presented in the present work were selected and translated from the traditions left by the foremost exponents of Islam. They include expositions elucidating the principle of *tawḥīd* and making clear the fundamental basis of all Islamic sciences and pursuits. At the same time they contain excellent and subtle allusions to the manner in which the important remaining sciences are ordered and organized around *tawḥīd*, how the moral virtues are based upon it, and how finally the practical aspects of Islam are founded upon and derived from these virtues. Finally, ᶜAlī's "Instructions to Mālik al-Ashtar" clarify the general situation of Islamic society in relation to the practical application of Islamic government.

All the traditions translated in the present work are summarized in the following two sentences: "Islam is the religion of seeing things as they are" and "Islam means to submit to the Truth (*al-ḥaqq*) and to follow It in one's beliefs and actions."

ᶜAllāmah Sayyid Muḥammad Ḥusayn Ṭabāṭabā'ī

PART I

ON THE UNITY OF GOD

A follower of the Islamic religion must first accept the testimony of faith: "There is no god but God" (*lā ilāha illa-llāh*). This profession of God's Unity is Islam's first pillar (*rukn*). All else depends upon it and derives from it.

But what does it mean to say that there is no god but God? For Islam, the manner in which the believer answers this question displays the depth to which he understands his religion. And, paraphrasing a *ḥadīth* of the Prophet often quoted in Sufi texts, one might say that there are as many ways of understanding the meaning of this profession as there are believers.[1]

Islamic intellectual history can be understood as a gradual unfolding of the manner in which successive generations of men have understood the meaning and implications of professing God's Unity. Theology, jurisprudence, philosophy, Sufism, even to some degree the natural sciences, all seek to explain at some level the principle of *tawḥīd*, "To profess that God is One." Some of the most productive of the intellectual schools which have attempted to explain the meaning of *tawḥīd* have flourished among Shi'ites.

Many historians have looked outside of Islam to find the inspiration for Islam's philosophical and metaphysical expositions of the nature of God's Unity. Such scholars tend to relegate anything more than what could derive — that is, in their view — from a "simple bedouin faith" to outside influence. Invariably they ignore the rich treasuries of wisdom contained in the vast corpus of Shi'ite *ḥadīth* literature pertaining to Islam's first centuries, i.e., the sayings of the Imams who were the acknowledged authorities in the religious sciences not only by the Shi'ites but also by the Sunnis. Even certain sayings of the Prophet which provide inspiration for the Imams have been ignored. In particular, the great watershed of Islamic metaphysical teachings, ᶜAlī ibn Abī Ṭālib, the Prophet's cousin and son-in-law and the Shi'ites' first Imam, has been largely overlooked.

In the following selections from *Biḥār al-anwār*, fifteen out of hundreds that can be found in Shi'ite sources, the reader will see the seeds for much of later Islamic metaphysical speculation. It will be noticed that the style of the *ḥadīths* varies little from the Prophet himself to the eighth Imam, the last from whom large numbers of such sayings have been handed down. The most important sources for such *ḥadīths*, i.e., the Prophet, the first, fifth, sixth, seventh and eighth Imams, are all represented.

The basic themes of the selections remain largely constant. The Prophet and the Imams all emphasize God's transcendence, or His "incomparability" (*tanzīh*) with the creatures. We may speak of God — although only on the authority of His own words, i.e., the Quran — but the expressions we employ are not to be understood as they are when we use the same words to describe the creatures. At the same time, the very fact that words can properly be employed to refer to God show that in some respect He is indeed "comparable" or "similar" (*tashbīh*) to His creation, if only in the sense that His creation is somehow "similar" to Him because created by Him. Otherwise, the words employed to speak about Him would all be meaningless, or each one would be equivalent to every other. But this second dimension of God's Reality — one more emphasised in Sufism — is relatively ignored in favor of His incomparability. Another theme of the selections is man's inability to grasp God through such things as the powers of his reason and his senses. The constant emphasis upon this point underlines God's incomparability and illustrates the particular errors to which the polytheistic and anthropomorphic thinking and imagination of the "Age of Ignorance" (*al-jāhiliyyah*) before Islam was prone.

In order to clarify the meaning of the selections, I have tried to supply a sufficient number of annotations. To comment upon the sayings in detail has been the task of much of Shi'ite speculation throughout the centuries. Every word and every sentence have provided numerous scholars with ample opportunity to display their erudition. But for a Western audience, one can only hope to point out the most important references to the Quran and the prophetic *ḥadīth* literature — references which are largely obvious for the Arabic speaking Muslim. Then I have tried to illustrate the manner in which later commentators have elaborated upon the *ḥadīths* by quoting a number of explanatory passages, in Part I mostly from Majlisī, the compiler of the *Biḥār al-anwār*. Some of these commentaries are necessary to understand the bearing of the text, but others may seem to obscure an apparently obvious sentence. In the latter case, this is largely because the commentators usually try to explain the text by referring to theological and philosophical concepts familiar to their readers, but not so to the average Westerner. However that may be, such notes illustrate the manner in which later speculation has expanded and developed an aphoristic mode of expression into a complex metaphysical system.

A. The Prophet

1. Profession of Faith

Abū ᶜAbdallāh (the sixth Imam) has related from his fathers that the Prophet of God — God bless him and his household[2] — said in one of his sermons, "Praise belongs to God, who in His firstness (*awwaliyyah*) was solitary and in His beginninglessness (*azaliyyah*) was tremendously exalted through divinity and supremely great through His magnificence and power.[3] He originated that which He produced and brought into being that which He created without a model (*mithāl*) preceding anything that He created. Our Lord, the eternal (*al-qadīm*), unstitched (the heavens and the earth)[4] through the subtlety (*luṭf*) of His lordship and the knowledge within His omniscience, created all that He created through the laws of His power (*qudrah*), and split (the sky) through the light of dawn.[5] So none changes His creation, none alters His handiwork, 'none repels His law' (XIII, 45)[6], none rejects His command. There is no place of rest away from His call (*daᶜwah*),[7] no cessation to His dominion and no interruption of His term. He is the truly existent (*al-kaynūn*) from the first and the truly enduring (*al-daymūm*) forever. He is veiled from His creatures by His light in the high horizon, in the towering might, and in the lofty dominion. He is above all things and below all things. So He manifested Himself (*tajallā*) to His creation without being seen, and He transcends being gazed upon. He wanted to be distinguished by the profession of Unity (*tawḥīd*) when He withdrew behind the veil of His light, rose high in His exaltation and concealed Himself from His creation.[8]

"He sent to them messengers so they might be His conclusive argument against His creatures[9] and so His messengers to them might be witnesses against them.[10] He sent among them prophets bearing good tidings and warning, 'that whosoever perished might perish by a clear sign, and by a clear sign he might live who lived' (VIII, 42) and that the servants might understand of their Lord that of which they had been ignorant, recognize Him in His Lordship after they had denied (it) and profess His Unity in His divinity after they had stubbornly resisted."

2. *God's Attributes*

Ibn ᶜAbbās related that a Jew, called Naᶜthal, stood up before the Prophet of God — upon whom be blessings and peace — and said, "O Muhammad, verily I will ask thee about certain things which have been repeating themselves in my breast for some time. If thou answerest them for me I will embrace Islam at thy hand."

The Prophet said, "Ask, O Abū ᶜUmmārah!"

Then he said, "O Muhammad, describe for me thy Lord."

He answered, "Surely the Creator cannot be described except by that with which He has described Himself — and how should one describe that Creator whom the senses cannot perceive, imaginations cannot attain, thoughts (*khaṭarāt*) cannot delimit and sight cannot encompass? Greater is He than what the depicters describe! He is distant in His nearness and near in His distance. He fashions (*kayyaf*) 'howness' (*kayfiyyah*), so it is not said of Him, 'How?' (*kayf*); He determines (*ayyan*) the 'where' (*ayn*), so it is not said of Him, 'Where?' (*ayn*). He sunders 'howness' (*kayfūfiyyah*) and 'whereness' (*aynūniyyah*), so He is "One . . . . the Everlasting Refuge" (CXII, 1-2), as He has described Himself.

But depicters do not attain to His description. 'He has not begotten, and has not been begotten, and equal to Him is not any one' (CXII, 3-4).

Naᶜthal said, "Thou hast spoken the truth. O Muhammad, tell me about thy saying, 'Surely He is One, there is none like (*shabīh*) Him.' Is not God one and man one? And thus His oneness (*waḥdāniyyah*) resembles the oneness of man."

He answered, "God is one, but single in meaning (*aḥadī al-maᶜnā*), while man is one but dual in meaning (*thanawī al-maᶜnā*): corporeal substance (*jism*) and accidents (*ᶜaraḍ*), body (*badan*) and spirit (*rūḥ*). Similarity (*tashbīh*)[11] pertains only to the meanings."

Naᶜthal said, "Thou hast spoken the truth, O Muhammad."

B. ᶜAlī, the First Imam

1. The Transcendent Lord

It was related by ᶜAlī ibn Mūsā al-Riḍā (the eighth Imam) from the earlier Imams in succession that al-Ḥusayn ibn ᶜAlī (the third Imam) spoke as follows: The Commander of the Faithful — upon whom be peace — addressed the people in the mosque at Kufa and said:

"Praise belongs to God, who did not originate from anything, nor did He bring what exists into being from anything.[12] His beginninglessness is attested to by the temporality (*ḥudūth*) of things, His power by the impotence with which He has branded them, and His everlastingness (*dawām*) by the annihilation (*fanā'*) which He has forced upon them. No place is empty of Him that He might be perceived through localization (*ayniyyah*), no object (*shabaḥ*) is like Him that He might be described by quality (*kayfiyyah*), nor is He absent from anything that He might be known through situation (*ḥaythiyyah.*)[13]

"He is distinct (*mubā'in*) in attributes from all that He has originated, inaccessible to perception because of the changing essences He has created (in things),[14] and outside of all domination (*taṣarruf*) by changing states (*ḥālāt*) because of grandeur and tremendousness. Forbidden is His delimitation (*taḥdīd*) to the penetrating acumen of sagacities, His description (*takyīf*) to the piercing profundities of thought and His representation (*taṣwīr*) to the searching probes of insight.

"Because of His tremendousness places encompass Him not, because of His majesty measures guage Him not, and because of His grandeur standards judge Him not. Impossible is it for imaginations (*awhām*) to fathom Him, understandings (*afhām*) to comprehend Him or minds (*adhhān*) to imagine Him. Powers of reason (*ᶜuqūl*) with lofty aspiration despair of contriving to comprehend Him, oceans of knowledge run dry without alluding to Him in depth,[15] and the subtleties of disputants fall from loftiness to pettiness in describing His power.

"He is One (*wāḥid*), not in terms of number (*ᶜadad*); Everlasting (*dā'im*), without duration (*amad*); Standing (*qā'im*), without supports (*ᶜumud*). He is not of a kind (*jins*) that (other) kinds should be on a par with Him, nor an object that objects should be similar to Him, nor like things that attributes should apply to Him. Powers of reason go astray in the waves of the current of perceiving Him, imaginations are bewildered at encompassing the mention of His beginninglessness, understandings are held back from becoming conscious of the description of His power, and minds are drowned in the depths of the heavens of His kingdom (*malakūt*).[16]

"He is Master over (giving) bounties, Inaccessible through Grandeur, and Sovereign over all things. Time (*al-dahr*) makes Him not old, nor does description encompass Him. Humbled before Him are the firmest of obduracies in the limits of their constancy, and submitted to Him are the most unshakeable of the cords in the extremity of their towering regions.[17]

"Witness to His Lordship (*rubūbiyyah*) is the totality of kinds (*al-ajnās*, i.e., kinds of creatures), to His Power their incapacity, to His eternity (*qidmah*) their createdness (*fuṭūr*), and to His permanence (*baqā'*) their passing into extinction (*zawāl*). So they possess no place of refuge from His grasp (*idrāk*) of them, no exit from His encompassing (*iḥāṭah*) them, no way of veiling themselves from His enumeration (*iḥṣā'*) of them and no way of avoiding His power over them. Sufficient is the perfection of His making them[18] as a sign (*āyah*), His compounding of their (natural) constitutions as a proof, the temporal origin (*ḥudūth*) of their natures as (a reason for His) eternity, and the creation's laws governing them as a lesson.[19] No limit is attributed to Him, no similitude struck for Him and nothing veiled from Him. High indeed is He exalted above the striking of similitudes and above created attributes!

"And I testify that there is no god but He, having faith in His lordship and opposing whoso denies Him; and I testify that Muhammad is His servant and messenger, residing in the best lodging-place, having passed from the noblest of loins and immaculate wombs, extracted in lineage from the noblest of mines and in origin from the most excellent of plantations, and (derived) from the most inaccessible of summits and the most glorious roots, from the tree from which God fashioned His prophets and chose His trusted ones:[20] (a tree) of excellent wood, harmonious stature, lofty branches, flourishing limbs, ripened fruit, (and) noble interior, implanted in generosity and cultivated in a sacred precinct. There it put forth branches and fruit, became strong and unassailable, and then made him (the prophet Muhammad) tall and eminent, until God, the Mighty and Majestic, honored him with the Faithful Spirit,[21] the Illuminating Light,[22] and the Manifest Book.[23] He subjected to him Burāq[24] and the angels greeted him.[25] By means of him He terrified the devils, overthrew the idols and the gods (who were) worshipped apart from Him. His prophet's Wont (*sunnah*) is integrity (*rushd*), his conduct (*sīrah*) is justice and his decision is truth. He proclaimed that which was commanded by his Lord,[26] and he delivered that with which he was charged[27] until he made plain his mission through the profession of Unity and made manifest among the creatures that there is no god but God alone and that He has no associate; until His Oneness became pure and His lordship unmixed. God made manifest his argument through the profession of His Unity and He raised his degree with submission (*al-islām*). And God, the Mighty and Majestic, chose for His prophet what was with Him of repose, degree and means — upon him and upon his pure household be God's peace."

2. *Via negativa*

ᶜAlī said, "Praise belongs to God, whose laudation is not rendered by speakers,[28] whose bounties are not counted by reckoners,[29] and whose rightfully due (*ḥaqq*) is not discharged by those who strive. Grand aspirations perceive Him not and deep-diving perspicacities reach Him not. His attributes (*ṣifah*) possess no determined limits (*ḥadd maḥdūd*), no existing description (*naᶜt mawjūd*), no fixed time (*waqt maᶜdūd*) and no extended term (*ajal mamdūd*). He originates the creatures by His power,[30] looses the winds by His mercy,[31] and fastens the shaking of His earth with boulders.[32]

"The first step in religion is knowledge (*maᶜrifah*) of Him. The perfection of knowledge of Him is to confirm Him (*taṣdīq*). The perfection of confirming Him is to profess His unity (*tawḥīd*). The perfection of professing His Unity is sincerity (*ikhlāṣ*) towards Him.[33] And the perfection of sincerity towards Him is to negate attributes (*nafy al-ṣifāt*) from Him, because of the testimony of every attribute that it is not that which possesses the attribute (*al-mawṣūf*) and the testimony of everything that possesses attributes that it is not the attribute.

"So whoso describes God — glory be to Him — has given Him a comrade (i.e. the description). Whoso gives Him a comrade has declared Him to be two (*tathniyah*). Whoso declares Him to be two has divided Him. Whoso divides Him is ignorant of Him. (Whoso is ignorant of Him points to Him).[34] Whoso points to Him has delimited Him. Whoso delimits Him has numbered Him. Whoso says, 'In what is He?', has enclosed Him. Whoso says, 'On what is He?', has excluded Him (from certain things).

"He is a being (*kā'in*) not as the result of temporal origin (*ḥadath*), an existent (*mawjūd*) not (having come) from non-existence (*ᶜadam*). He is with everything, not through association (*muqāranah*); and He is other than everything, not through separation (*muzāyalah*). He is active (*fāᶜil*), not in the sense of possessing movement and instruments. He was seeing when there was none of His creatures to be observed by Him. He was 'alone' (*mutawaḥḥid*) when there was none with whom to be intimate and at whose loss to feel lonely.

"He originated creation and gave to it its beginning without employing deliberation, profiting from experience, occasioning movement (*ḥarakah*, i.e. in Himself), or being disrupted by the cares of the soul (*hamāmah nafs*). He delays things to their times,[35] mends their discrepancies, implants (in them) their natural dispositions, and makes these (dispositions) adhere to their objects. He has knowledge of them before their beginning, encompasses their limits (*ḥudūd*) and their end (*intihā'*) and knows their relationships (*qarā'in*) and aspects (*aḥnā'*)."

3. Firm Rooting in Knowledge

It was related from Abū ᶜAbdallāh that when the Commander of the Faithful was speaking from the pulpit at Kufa a man stood up and said, "O Commander of the Faithful! Describe for us thy Lord — blessed and transcendent is He — that our love (*ḥubb*) for Him and knowledge (*maᶜrifah*) of Him may increase."

The Commander of the Faithful became angry and cried out, "Assemble for prayer!" The people gathered together until the mosque was choked with them. Then he stood, his color changing, and he said, "Praise belongs to God, who does not gain in plenty by withholding nor become poor through giving, while every other giver than He diminishes. (He is) full of the benefits of blessings and the advantages of superabundance. Through His generosity He ensures the provision of creatures. So He smooths the path of aspiration (*ṭalab*) for those who make Him their Quest. Nor is He more generous with what is asked of Him than with what is not asked. Time in its march varies not for Him that (His) state should change accordingly. If He should give to some of His servants (all of) the silver metal, ingots of pure gold and sacks of pearls that the mountains' mines breathe[36] and the seas' shells smile, His generosity would in nowise be affected, nor would the expanse of that which is with Him dwindle. With Him are treasuries of bounteous bestowal which are not exhausted by objects of request and which come not to His attention in spite of their abundance, for He is the Generous who is not diminished by gifts nor made niggardly by the importunity of the importune. And 'His command, when He desires a thing, is to say to it "Be", and it is' (XXXVI, 81).

"The angels, despite their proximity to the throne of His liberality, the great extent of their burning love (*walah*) for Him, (their) glorification of the majesty of His might, and their proximity to the unseen of His kingdom (*ghayb malakūtih*), are capable of knowing only what He has taught them of His affair, although they are of the Sacred Kingdom in terms of rank. It is because they possess knowledge of Him only as He created them that they say, 'Glory be to Thee! We know not save what Thou hast taught us' (II, 32).[37]

"So what is thy opinion, O questioner, of Him who is thus? Glory be to Him, and praise belongs to Him! He has not come into being that change or removal should be possible in Him. He is not affected in His Essence by recurrence of states, and aeons of nights and days differ not for Him. (It is He) who originated creation with no model (*mithāl*) to copy or measure (*miqdār*) to imitate from a deity (*maᶜbūd*) who should have existed before Him. Attributes encompass Him not, lest He be defined by limits (*ḥudūd*) (resulting) from their having attained Him. He — 'like Him there is naught' (XLII, 11) — never ceases to transcend the attributes of creatures.

"Eyes are prevented from reaching Him, lest He be described through being plainly seen (*bi-l-ᶜiyān*) and lest He be known among His creatures in the Essence that none knows but He. Through His exaltation (*ᶜuluww*) over things He eludes that upon which falls the conjectures of imaginers (*mutawahhimīn*). The inmost center (*kunh*) of His tremendousness transcends the embrace of the impotent deliberation of those who meditate. He has no similitude that what is created should resemble Him. For those who have knowledge of Him He is forever above likenesses and opposites.

"Those who ascribe rivals to God (*al-ᶜādilūn billāh*) cry lies when they make Him similar to the like of their categories, adorn Him in their imaginations with the adornment of creatures, divide Him with a measure resulting from the notions of their concerns, and measure Him by the talents of their reason's powers[38] in terms of the creatures with their multiple faculties. For how should the deliberations of imaginations assess Him whose measure cannot be determined, when surely the notions of understanding have erred in conceiving of His inmost center? For He is greater than that the minds of men should delimit Him through thought (*tafkīr*) or angels should encompass Him through estimation, despite their proximity to the kingdom of His might.

"High be He exalted above having an equal (*kufw*) with which to be compared, for He is the Subtle: when imaginations desire to encroach upon Him in the depths of the unseen regions of His dominion, (when) thoughts (*fikar*) free from insinuating intrusions seek to grasp knowledge of His Essence, (when) hearts are thrown into mad confusion over Him in trying to embrace Him through conforming to His attributes, (when) the ways of approach of reason's powers become obscured since no attributes attain to Him by which they might gain the knowledge of His divinity, (then) they (imaginations, thoughts, hearts and ways of approach) are checked in disgrace while traversing the chasms of the dark reaches of the unseen worlds, rid (of all things) for Him — glory be to Him! They return having been thrown back, admitting that the inmost center of His knowledge is not reached through the deviation of straying (from the path)[39] and that no notion of the measure of His might's majesty occurs to the mind of meditators, by reason of His distance from being (encompassed) within the faculties of limited beings. For He is counter to (*khilāf*) His creation, and there is nothing like Him among creatures. Now a thing is only compared with its like (*ᶜadīl*). As for what has no like, how should it be compared with what is other than its like (*mithāl*)? And He is the Beginning (*al-badī'*) before whom was naught, and the Last (*al-ākhir*) after whom will be naught.

"Eyes reach Him not in the splendor of His Power (*jabarūt*). When He obscures them with veils, eyes do not penetrate the density of the veils' thickness, nor do they pierce the firmness pertaining to His coverings to (reach) the 'Possessor of the Throne',[40] in whose will affairs originate and before the majesty of whose tremendousness the grandeur of the arrogant cringes. Necks are bowed before Him and faces humbled in fear of Him. In the marvels (*badā'iᶜ*) which He creates appear the traces (*āthār*) of His wisdom (*ḥikmah*), and all that is created becomes an argument (*ḥujjah*) for Him and attributed to Him. Were it a silent creation His argument would be speaking through it in His directing (of its affairs, *tadbīr*).[41]

"He determines what He creates and makes firm His determining (*taqdīr*), places everything in its place through the subtlety of His directing, and turns it in a direction.[42] Then nothing of it reaches the environs of His station.[43] It falls not short before carrying out His will and refrains not when ordered to execute His desire. He suffers not from weariness that might touch Him,[44] nor is He deceived by one who would transgress His command.[45]

"So His creation is complete and it yields to Him in obedience. It complies with the (appointed) time at which He brings it forth, a response resisted by neither the dawdler's hesitation nor the lingerer's tardiness. He straightened the crookedness of things, delineated the way-marks of their limits, reconciled their contradictions through His power, joined the means of their conjunctions (*asbāb qarā'inihā*), caused their various sorts to be disparate in size, and divided them into different kinds, natural dispositions, and appearances — marvels of creation, whose fashioning He made firm. He made them according to His desire and[46] brought them into existence. His knowledge put in order the kinds of their creation and His directing achieved their fairest determination.

"O questioner! Know that whoso compares our majestic Lord to the mutual dissimilarity of the parts of His creation and to the interconnection of their joints, hidden by the directing of His wisdom, surely he has not fixed his inmost consciousness (*ghayb ḍamīrih*) upon knowledge of Him, and his heart has not witnessed (*mushāhadah*) the certainty that He has no compeer. It is as if he had not heard of the followers disclaiming the followed, saying, 'By God, we were certainly in manifest error when we made you equal to the Lord of all beings' (XXVI, 97-8).[47]

"Whoso sets our Lord equal to something has ascribed rivals to Him, and he who ascribes rivals to Him is a disbeliever in what His clear verses[48] have revealed and in what the witnesses of His clear signs' arguments have spoken. For He is God, who does not become defined within the powers of reason that He should be qualified within the range of their thought or be limited and turned about within the craws of the reflection of aspiring souls.[49] He is the Producer of the kinds of things without having been in need of reflection, or of acting according to an innate disposition, or of experience gained through the passing of Time's events, or of an associate to help Him in bringing into existence the wonders of affairs. When those who ascribe rivals to Him compare Him to creation, whose attributes are divided and limited and whose levels possess various zones and regions — and He, the Mighty and Majestic, is the existent through Himself, not through His instruments (*adāh*) — they can not have measured Him with His true measure. Thus He said, declaring Himself incomparable with the association of compeers and rising above the estimate of those of His disbelieving servants who measure Him within limits, 'They measure not God with His true measure. The earth altogether shall be His handful on the Day of Resurrection, and the heavens shall be rolled up in His right hand. Glory be to Him!

High be He exalted above that they associate' (XXXIX, 67).

"So as for that to which the Quran directs thee concerning His attributes, follow it, so that a link may be established between thee and knowledge (*ma^crifah*) of Him. Take it as an example, and seek illumination by the light of its guidance; surely it is a blessing and a wisdom given to thee, so take what has been given thee and be among the thankful.[50] But as for that to which Satan directs thee, that which is not made encumbent upon thee in the Quran and no trace (*athar*) concerning which exists in the Wont of the Prophet and the Imams of guidance, leave its knowledge to God, the Mighty and Majestic. Surely that is the limit of God's claim (*ḥaqq*) against thee.

"Know that 'those firmly rooted in knowledge'[51] are they whom God has freed from the need to assault the closed doors beyond which are the unseen things (*al-ghuyūb*), so they cling to the acknowledgement (*iqrār*) of all of the veiled unseen of which they know not the interpretation, and they say, 'We have faith in it; all is from our Lord.' (III, 7). So God praised their avowal of incapacity to grasp what they comprehend not in knowledge, and He called their abandonment of the desire to penetrate into that whose examination is not required of them 'firm-rootedness'. So limit thyself to that (same attitude) and measure not the Mightiness of God — Glory be to Him — according to the measure of thy reason's power, thus becoming of those who perish."

4. *The Fairest of Creators*

It has been related that ᶜAlī — upon whom be peace — delivered the following sermon at Kufa. He was standing on a stone that had been set up for him by Jaᶜdah ibn Hubayrah al-Makhzūmī.[52] He wore an outer garment of wool. His sword belt and his shoes were made of fiber. His forehead was like the knee of a camel.[53] He said, "Praise belongs to God, unto whom are the homecomings of creation and the issues of the affair.[54] We praise Him for His mighty goodness, His radiant proof (*burhān*) and the profusion of His bounty and gracious giving; a praise which might render Him His rightfully due, accomplish His thanks, bring (us) near to His reward and cause the fairest of His increase.[55] We pray to Him for succour,[56] the prayer of one hoping for His bounty, anticipating

His benefit, having confidence in Him to avert (evil), acknowledging His blessings and submitting to Him in deed and word. We believe in Him with the faith (*īmān*) of one who hopes for Him with certainty, turns to Him as a believer, humbles himself before Him in submission, sincerely professes His Unity (*akhlaṣ muwaḥḥidan*), magnifies Him in glorification and seeks refuge in Him, desiring and striving (*rāghiban mujtahidan*).

" 'He has not been begotten' (CXII, 3) — glory be to Him — that He should share in Might, and 'He has not begotten' (CXII, 3) that He should bequeath and perish. Time (*waqt*) precedes Him not, nor duration, and increase and decrease seize Him not by turns.

"Nay, He appears to the powers of reason by the marks He has shown us of (His) perfect directing and certain decree. So of the witnesses of His creation is the creation of the heavens without pillars,[57] standing without supports. He called them and they answered, obeying, submissive, without hesitation or delay.[58] Had it not been for their acknowledging (*iqrār*) Him in lordship and their willing submission (to Him), He would not have appointed them the locus of His Throne, nor the dwelling place for His angels, nor the place of ascent of good words and the righteous deed of His creation.[59] He appointed their stars waymarks by which the bewildered traveller is guided in the divergent paths of the lands. The thickness of the dark night's curtain prevents not the shining of their light, and the garments of the black night's blackness cannot push back the brilliance of the light of the moon that spreads in the heavens.

"So glory be to Him, from whom is not hidden the blackness of a gloomy dusk or still night in the hollows of lands low, nor in the peaks of neighboring mountains;[60] (nor) that with which the thunder reverberates in the horizon of heaven; (nor) that from which the lightning of the clouds vanishes;[61] (nor) the leaf which falls, removed from its place of falling by the gales caused by the stars (*al-anwā'*)[62] and the pouring down of the rain. He knows the place where the raindrop falls and where it takes its rest, the route by which the tiny ant draws and drags (on the ground), what is sufficient food for a gnat[63] and what the female bears within her womb.[64]

"Praise belongs to God, the Existent (*al-kā'in*) before there was a Pedestal (*kursī*), or Throne (*ʿarsh*), or heaven, or earth, or jinn, or man. He is not perceived by imagination (*wahm*) or measured by understanding (*fahm*). Petitioners busy Him not[65] and giving diminishes Him not. He is not observed by eyes, nor delimited by location ("where", *ayn*), nor described by pairs.[66] He creates not through application'[67] is perceived not by the senses and is compared not with man.

"He it is who spoke to Moses directly[68] and showed him one of His mighty signs'[69] without members (*jawāriḥ*), instruments (*adawāt*), speech or throat.[70] Nay, if thou speakest truly, O thou who affectest to describe thy Lord, then describe Gabriel, Michael and the hosts of the angels brought nigh, bowing in the sacred chambers (*ḥujarāt al-quds*), their intellects in adoring perplexity to delimit the 'Fairest of Creators'.[71] Surely only those are perceived through attributes who possess forms and instruments and who end in annihilation when they reach the limit of their term. There is no god but He. He illumines with His Light every darkness and He darkens with His Darkness every light."

5. *Oneness*

It has been related that on the day of the Battle of the Camel[72] a bedouin came before the Commander of the Faithful and said, "O Commander of the Faithful! Sayest thou that God is one?"

The people attacked him and said, "O bedouin! Doest thou not see how the Commander of the Faithful's heart is divided (with cares)?"

The Commander of the Faithful said, "Leave him, for surely what the bedouin wishes (i.e., knowledge of God) is what we wish for the people." Then he said, "O bedouin! To say that God is one (*wāḥid*) has four (possible) meanings, two of which are not permissible concerning God, the Mighty and Majestic, and two of which are established concerning Him.

"As for the two which are not permissible concerning Him, (the first is) the saying of him who says 'one' and has in mind the category of numbers. Now this is not permissible, for that which has no second does not enter into the category of numbers. Hast thou not seen that he who says that He is 'the third of three'[73] is of the unbelievers? And (the second is like) the saying of him who says (concerning a man), 'He is one of mankind', meaning that he is one kind within the species.[74] This is not permissible because it is a comparison, and our Lord is greater than that and high above it.

"As for the two meanings which are established concerning Him, (the first is) the saying of him who says, 'He is one, there is no likeness (*shabah*) unto Him among things.' Such is our Lord. And (the second is) the saying of him who says, 'Surely He, the Mighty and Majestic, is single in meaning (*aḥadī al-maᶜnā*), intending by that that He is not divided by existence, the power of reason, or imagination.[75] Such is our Lord, the Mighty and Majestic."[76]

6. *Discernment*

In another sermon ᶜAlī — upon whom be peace — said, "What points to Him (*dalīluh*) is His signs (*āyāt*);[77] to perceive Him (*wujūduh*) is to affirm Him (*ithbātuh*);[78] to know Him is to profess His unity; and professing His Unity is to distinguish Him (*tamyīz*) from His creation. The standard (*ḥukm*) for distinguishing is separation (*baynūnah*) in attribute, not separation in terms of distance (*ᶜuzlah*). Surely He is a creating Lord (*rabb khāliq*), neither possessing a Lord nor created. Whatever can be conceived of is different from Him."

Then after that he said, "Whoso is known in himself (*bi-nafsihi*) is not a god: this is the guide to that which points to Him (*al-dalīl ᶜalayh*) and this it is which leads to knowledge of Him."

7. *The Vision of the Heart*

Abū ᶜAbdallāh related as follows: the Commander of the Faithful was speaking from the pulpit at Kufa when a man called Dhiᶜlib stood up before him. He was sharp-tongued, eloquent and courageous. He said, "O Commander of the Faithful! Hast thou seen thy Lord?"

He said, "Woe unto thee, O Dhiᶜlib! I would not be worshipping a lord whom I have not seen."

He said, "O Commander of the Faithful! How didst thou see Him?"

He answered, "O Dhiᶜlib! Eyes see Him not through sight's

observation, but hearts see Him through the verities of faith (*ḥaqā'iq al-īmān*). Woe to thee, O Dhiᶜlib! Verily, my Lord is subtle in subtlety (*laṭif al-laṭāfah*), but He is not described by subtleness (*luṭf*); tremendous in tremendousness (*ᶜaẓīm al-ᶜaẓamah*), but not described by tremendousness (*ᶜiẓam*); grand in grandeur (*kabīr al-kibriyā'*), but not described by grandness (*kibr*); and majestic in majesty (*jalīl al-jalālah*), but not described by greatness (*ghilaẓ*). Before all things He was; it is not said that anything was before Him. After all things He will be; it is not said that He possesses an 'after'.[79] He willed (all) things, not through resolution (*himmah*). He is all-perceiving (*darrāk*), not through any artifice (*khadīᶜah*). He is in all things, but not mixed (*mutamāzij*) with them, nor separate (*bā'in*) from them. He is Outward (*ẓāhir*), not according to the explanation of being immediate (to the senses: *mubāsharah*); Manifest (*mutajallin*), not through the appearance of a vision (of Him: *istihlāl ru'yah*); Separate, not through distance (*masāfah*); Near (*qarīb*), not through approach (*mudānāh*); Subtle, not through corporealization (*tajassum*); Existent (*mawjūd*), not after nonexistence (*ᶜadam*); Active (*fāᶜil*), not through coercion (*iḍṭirār*); Determining (*muqaddir*), not through movement (*ḥarakah*); Desiring (*murīd*), not through resolution (*hamāmah*); Hearing (*samīᶜ*), not through means (*ālah*); and Seeing (*baṣīr*), not through organs (*adāh*).[80]

"Spaces (*amākin*) encompass Him not, times (*awqāt*) accompany Him not, attributes (*ṣifāt*) delimit Him not and slumbers (*sināt*) seize Him not.[81]

"By His giving sense (*tashᶜīr*) to sense organs (*mashāᶜir*) it is known that He has no sense organs.[82] By His giving substance (*tajhīr*) to substances (*jawāhir*) it is known that He has no substance.[83] By His causing opposition (*muḍāddah*) among things it is known that He has no opposite (*ḍidd*).[84] By His causing affiliation (*muqāranah*) among affairs it is known that He has no affiliate (*qarīn*). He opposed darkness to light, obscurity to clarity, moisture to solidity,[85] and heat to cold. He joins together those things which are hostile to one another, and separates those which are near. They prove (the existence of) their Separator (*mufarriq*) by their separation and their Joiner (*mu'allif*) by their junction. This is (the meaning of) His words — He is the Mighty and Majestic — 'And of everything created We two kinds; haply you will remember' (LI, 49).

"So through them He separated 'before' and 'after' that it might be known that He has no before and after. They testify with their temperaments (*gharā'iz*) that He who gave them temperaments has no temperament. They announce through their subjection to time (*tawqīt*) that He who has subjected them to time is not subject to it Himself.

"He veiled some of them from others so that it might be known that there is no veil between Him and His creation other than His creation. He was a Lord when there was none over whom He was Lord (*marbūb*); a God when there was none for whom to be a God (*ma'lūh*); a Knower (*ᶜālim*) when there was nothing to be known (*maᶜlūm*); and a Hearer when there was nothing to be heard (*masmūᶜ*)."

Then ᶜAlī composed the following verses extemporaneously:

"My Lord is ever known by praise, my Lord is ever described by generosity.

"He was, when there was no light by which to seek illumination, and no darkness bent over the horizons.

"So our Lord is counter to creatures, all of them, and to all that is described in imaginations.

"Whoso desires Him portrayed through comparison returns beleagured, shackled by his incapacity,

"And in the Ascending Stairways the wave of His power casts a wave which blinds the eye of the spirit.[86]

"So abandon the quarreler in religion lost in the depths, for in him doubt has corrupted his view.

"And become the companion of that reliable one who is the beloved of his Master and surrounded by the favors of his Protector:

"Smiling, he became in the earth the waymark of guidance (*dalīl al-hudā*) and in Heaven the adorned and acknowledged."

After this Dhiᶜlib fell to the ground in a faint. When he recovered he said, "I have never heard such words. I will not return to any of that (which I believed before)."

C. al-Bāqir, the Fifth Imam

The Incomparable Lord

Abū Baṣīr has related that a man came to Abū Jaᶜfar (the fifth

Imam) and said to him, "O Abū Jaᶜfar, tell me about thy Lord! When was He?"

He said, "Woe unto thee! Surely it is said of a thing that was not, and *then* was, 'When was it?' But my Lord — blessed is He and high exalted — was ever-living without 'how' and had no 'was'. His Being (*kawn*) had no 'how', nor had it any 'where'. He was not in anything, nor was He on anything. He did not bring into existence a place (*makān*) for His Being (*kān*). He increased not in strength *after* bringing things into being, nor was He weak *before* bringing things into being. And He was not lonely (*mustawḥish*) before creating things. He resembles nothing brought into being. He was not devoid of power over the dominion before its production that He should be devoid of the dominion[87] after its passing. He remains Living without (created) life, a powerful King before He produces anything (over which to rule) and an all-compelling King (*malik jabbār*) after He produces the universe (*al-kawn*). His Being has no 'how', nor has it any 'where', nor has it any limit. He is not known through anything resembling Him. He ages not through the duration of His subsistence. He is thunderstruck by nothing. Nothing causes Him to fear. And all things are thunderstruck by fear of Him.[88]

"He is Living without temporal life, without a being (*kawn*) described by attributes, without a state which can be defined (*kayf maḥdūd*), without a trace which can be followed, and without a place adjacent to anything. Nay, He is a Living One who knows, a King who ever is. His are the power and the dominion. He produces what He wills through His will (*mashiyyah*). He is neither limited nor divided into parts, and He perishes not. He was the First, without 'how', and He will be the Last, without 'where'. And 'All things perish, except His Face' (XXVIII, 88). 'His are the creation and the command. Blessed be God, the Lord of all beings!' (VII, 54).

"Woe upon thee, O questioner! As for my Lord, truly imaginations envelop Him not, uncertainties touch Him not, He is oppressed by none, none is adjacent to Him, phenomena touch Him not, He is questioned not as to anything He does,[89] He comes not upon anything,[90] 'Slumber seizes Him not, neither sleep' (II, 255). 'To Him belongs all that is in the heavens and the earth and all that is between them, and all that is underneath the soil' (XX, 6)."

D. Jaᶜfar al-Ṣādiq, the Sixth Imam

1. Seeing God

Abū Baṣīr has related that he said to Abū ᶜAbdallāh — upon whom be peace — "Tell me about God, the Mighty and Majestic. Will believers see Him on the Day of Resurrection?"

He answered, "Yes, and they have already seen Him before the Day of Resurrection."

Abū Baṣīr asked, "When?"

The Imam answered, "When He said to them, 'Am I not your Lord?' They said: 'Yea, verily' (VII, 172)."[91] Then he was quiet for a time. Then he said, "Truly the believers see him in this world before the Day of Resurrection. Doest thou not see Him now?"

Abū Baṣīr then said to him, "That I might be made thy sacrifice! Shall I relate this (to others) from thee?"

He answered, "No, for if thou relatest it, a denier ignorant of the meaning of what thou sayest will deny it. Then he will suppose that it is comparison and unbelief (*kufr*). But seeing with the heart (*al-ru'yah b-il-qalb*) is not like seeing with the eyes (*al-ru'yah bi-l-ᶜayn*). High be God exalted above what the comparers (*mushabbihūn*) and heretics (*mulḥidūn*) describe!"

2. The name that can be named...

It has been related that Abū ᶜAbdallāh said, "The name of God is other than God, and everything that can be called by the name of a 'thing' (*shay'*)[92] is created, except God. Therefore all that tongues express or is worked by hands[93] is created. God is the goal of him who sets Him as his goal, but the determined goal (*al-mughayyā*, i.e., in the mind of man) is other than the (real) goal.[94] The goal possesses attributes (*mawṣūf*), and all that possesses attributes has been fashioned (*maṣnūᶜ*). But the Fashioner (*ṣāniᶜ*) of things does not possess the attributes of any stated limit (*ḥadd musammā*). He has not come into being that His Being (*kaynūnah*) should be known through fashioning (*ṣunᶜ*) (carried out) by other than He.[95] He does not terminate at a limit unless it be other than He. Whoso understands this principle (*ḥukm*) will never fall into error. It is the unadulterated profession of Unity (*al-tawḥīd al-khāliṣ*), so believe in it, confirm it, and understand it well, with God's permission — the Mighty and Majestic.

"Whoso maintains that he knows God by means of a veil (*ḥijāb*) or a form (*ṣurāh*) or a likeness (*mithāl*) is an associator (*mushrik*), for the veil, the likeness and the form are other than He. He is utterly and only One. So how should he who maintains that he knows Him by means of other than Him be professing Unity? Surely He alone knows God who knows Him by means of God (*billāh*). Therefore, whoso knows Him not by means of Him knows Him not. On the contrary, he only knows other than Him. There is nothing between the Creator and the created.[96] God is the Creator of things, but not from something. He is *named* by His names, so He is other than His names, and His names are other than He.[97] The described (*al-mawṣūf*) is other than the describer (*al-wāṣif*).

"Then whoso maintains that he has faith in that which he does not know has gone astray from knowledge (*maᶜrifah*).[98] A created thing (*makhlūq*) perceives nothing unless by means of God: the knowledge of God is perceived only by means of God. But God is empty of His creatures and His creatures are empty of Him.[99] When He desires a thing, it is as He desires, by His command (*amr*) and without speech (*nuṭq*). His servants have no refuge from that which He decrees (*mā qaḍā*), and they have no argument against that which is His pleasure. They have no power to act or to deal with that which is brought about in their bodies, created (by God), except by means of their Lord. So whoso maintains that he is able to perform an act which God, the Mighty and Majestic, does not desire, has maintained that his will (*irādah*) prevails over the Will of God. 'Blessed be God' the Lord of all beings!" (VII, 54.

E. Mūsā, the Seventh Imam

God's Might and Majesty

It has been related that the righteous servant, Mūsā ibn Jaᶜfar, said, "Surely God — there is no god but He — was the Living without 'how' (*kayf*) or 'where' (*ayn*). He was not in anything, nor was He on anything. He did not create a place (*makān*) for His grandeur (*makān*).[100] He increased not in might after bringing things into being. Nothing brought into being resembles Him. He was not devoid of power over the dominion before its production, nor will He be devoid of power (over it) after its passing.[101]

"He — the Mighty and Majestic — is a Living God without temporal life, King before He produces anything, Master after its production (*inshā'*). God has no limits (*ḥadd*). He is not known through something resembling Him. He ages not through subsistence (*baqā'*). He is struck not by fear of anything, and by fright before Him all things are thunderstruck.[102] So God is Living without temporal life, without a being described by attributes, without a state which can be defined, without a designated location or fixed place. Nay, He is Living in Himself, a Master whose power does not remove. He produced what He wills when He wills through His will and His power. He was First, without 'how', and will be Last, without 'where'. And 'All things perish, except His face' (XXVIII, 88). 'His are the creation and the command. Blessed be God, the Lord of all beings!' (VII, 54)."

F. ᶜAlī al-Riḍā, the Eighth Imam

1. *Profession of Unity*

It has been related that when al-Ma'mūn[103] desired to install al-Riḍā (as his successor), he collected together Banū Hāshim [104] and said to them, "Verily I desire to install al-Riḍā in this affair after me."

Banū Hāshim envied al-Riḍā and said, "Thou appointest an ignorant man who possesses not the insight to direct the caliphate. Therefore send for him. He will come to us and thou wilt see how his ignorance decides thee against him." So he sent for him and he came. Banū Hāshim said to him, "O Abu-l-Ḥasan! Ascend the pulpit and display for us a sigh whereby we may worship God."

So he ascended the pulpit and sat for a long time, his head bowed in silence. Then he trembled a great trembling and stood up straight, praised and lauded God, and asked His blessing for His prophet and his household. Then he said, "The first element in the worship of God is knowledge of Him, the root (*aṣl*) of knowledge of Him is to profess His Unity (*tawḥīd*), and the correct way (*niẓām*) to profess the Unity of God is to negate attributes from Him. For the powers of reason testify that every attribute and everything possessing an attribute (*mawṣūf*) is created. Everything possessing an attribute testifies that it has a Creator which is neither attribute nor possesses an attribute. Every attribute and everything possessing an attribute testify to connection (*iqtirān*, between the attribute and that to which it is attributed). Connection testifies to temporality (*ḥadath*). And temporality testifies that it accepts not the Beginningless, which accepts not the temporal.

"So it is not *God* whose Essence is known through comparison. It is not *His* Unity that is professed by someone who attempts to fathom Him. It is not *His* reality (*ḥaqīqah*) that is attained by someone who strikes a similitude for Him. It is not *He* who is confirmed (*taṣdīq*) by him who professes an end for Him. It is not *He* to whom repairs he who points to Him. It is not *He* who is meant by him who compares Him (to something). It is not to *Him* that he who divides Him into parts humbles himself. And it is not *He* who is desired by him who conceives of Him in his imagination.

"Everything that can be known in itself (*bi-nafsihi*) is fashioned (*maṣnūᶜ*).[105] All that stands apart from Him is an effect (*maᶜlūl*). God is inferred from what He fashions (*ṣunᶜ*), the knowledge of Him is made fast by the powers of reason, and the argument (*ḥujjah*) for Him is established by (man's) primordial nature (*al-fiṭrah*).

"God's creating of the creatures is a veil between Him and them. His separation (*mubāyanah*) from them is that He is disengaged from their localization (*ayniyyah*).[106] That He is their origin (*ibtidā'*) is proof for them that He has no origin, for none that has an origin can originate others. That He has created them possessing means (of accomplishing things) is proof that He has no means (*adāh*), for means are witness to the poverty of those who use them.

"So His names are an expression (*taᶜbīr*), His acts (*afᶜāl*) are (a way) to make (Him) understood (*tafhīm*), and His Essence is Reality (*ḥaqīqah*).[107] His inmost center (*kunh*) separates (*tafrīq*) Him from creation, and His otherness (*ghuyūr*) limits (*taḥdīd*) what is other than He. Therefore ignorant of God is he who asks for Him to be described! Transgressing against Him is he who seeks to encompass Him! Mistaken is he who imagines to have fathomed Him!

"Whoso says 'how?' has compared Him (to something). Whoso says 'why?' has professed for Him a cause (*taᶜlīl*). Whoso says 'when?' has determined Him in time (*tawqīt*). Whoso says 'in what?' has enclosed Him (*taḍmīn*). Whoso says 'to what?' has professed for Him a limit (*tanhiyah*). Whoso says 'until what?' has given Him an end (*taghiyah*). Whoso gives Him an end has associated an end with Him. Whoso associates an end with Him has divided Him. Whoso divides Him has described Him. Whoso describes Him has deviated from the straight path (*ilḥād*) concerning Him.[108]

"God does not change with the changes undergone by creation, just as He does not become limited by delimiting (*taḥdīd*) that which is limited (*al-maḥdūd*). He is One (*aḥad*), not according to the explanation offered by number (*ta'wīl ᶜadad*); Outward, not according to the explanation of being immediate (to the senses);[109] Manifest, not through the appearance of a vision (of Him); Inward (*bāṭin*), not through separation (*muzāyalah*); Apart (*mubā'in*), not through distance; Near, not through approach; Subtle, not through corporealization; Existent, not after non-existence; Active, not through coercion; Determining, not through the activity of thought (*jawl fikrah*); Directing (*mudabbir*), not through movement; Desiring, not through resolution; Willing (*shā'*), not through directing attention (*himmah*);[110] Grasping (*mudrik*), not through touch (*majāssah*); Hearing, not through means; and Seeing, not through organs.

"Times accompany Him not, places enclose Him not, slumber seizes Him not, attributes delimit Him not, and instruments (*adawāt*) are of no use to Him. His being (*kawn*) precedes times (*al-awqāt*), His existence (*wujūd*) non-existence and His beginninglessness (*azal*) beginning (*al-ibtidā'*).

"By His giving sense to the sense organs it is known that He has no sense organs. By His giving substance to substances it is known that He has no substance. By His causing opposition among things it is known that He has no opposite. By His causing affiliation among affairs it is known that He has no affiliate. He opposed darkness to light, obscurity to clarity, moisture to solidity, and heat to cold. He joins together those things which are hostile to one another and separates those which are near. They prove (the existence of) their Separator by their separation and their Joiner by their junction. That is (the meaning of) His words — He is the Mighty and Majestic — 'And of everything created We two kinds; haply you will remember' (LI, 49).

"So through them He separated 'before' and 'after' that it might be known that He has no before and after. They testify with their temperaments that He who gave them temperaments has no temperament. They prove by their disparity (*tafāwut*) that He who made them disparate has no disparity. They announce through their subjection to time that He who subjected them to time is not subject to it Himself.

"He veiled some of them from others so that it might be known that there is no veil between Him and them other than them. His is the meaning of lordship (*al-rubūbiyyah*) when there was none over whom He was Lord, the reality of godhood (*al-ilāhiyyah*) when there was nothing for whom He was God, the meaning of Knower when there was nothing to be known, the meaning of Creator (*khāliq*) when there was nothing created (*makhlūq*) and the import of hearing when there was nothing to be heard. It is not because He created that He deserves the meaning (of the term) 'Creator' and not because He brought the creatures into being that the meaning of 'making' is derived.

"How (should it not be so)? For *mudh* ('ever since') conceals Him not, *qad* ('already')[111] brings Him not near, *laᶜalla* ('perhaps') veils Him not, *matā* ('when?') limits Him not in time, *ḥīn* ('at the time of') contains Him not, and *maᶜ* ('with') brings Him not into association.[112] Instruments (*adawāt*) limit only themselves and means (*ālah*) allude only unto their own like.[113] Their activities are found only in things.[114] *Mudh* withholds things from being eternal (*qidmah*), *qad* shields them from beginninglessness, and *law lā* ('if only') wards off perfection (*al-takmilah*).[115] Things become separate and prove (the existence of) their Separator. They become distinguished and prove their Distinguisher (*mubā'in*). Through them their Maker manifests Himself to the powers of reason. Through (these powers)[116] He becomes veiled to sight, to them imaginations appeal for a decision,[117] in them is substantiated (only) other than Him, from them is suspended the proof and through them He makes known to them the acknowledgement (*al-iqrār*).[118]

"Confirmation (*tasdīq*) of God is made fast by the powers of reason, and faith (*īmān*) in Him reaches perfectoin through acknowledgment. There is no religiosity (*diyānah*) except after knowledge (*maᶜrifah*), no knowledge except through sincerity (*ikhlāṣ*) and no sincerity along with comparison.[119] There is no negation (*nafy*) of comparison if there is affirmation (*ithbāt*) of attributes.[120]

"So nothing in creation is found in its Creator. All that is possible in it is impossible in its Maker. Movement (*ḥarakah*) and stillness (*sukūn*) do not affect Him. How should that which He effects (in others) have effect upon Him, or that which He has originated recur for Him? Then His Essence would be disparate, His inmost center divided, His signification (*maᶜnā*) prevented from eternity. How would the Creator have a meaning different from the created?

"If something from behind limited Him, then something in front would limit Him. If perfection (*tamām*) were seeking Him, imperfection would be upon Him. How should that which does not transcend (*imtināᶜ*) temporality be worthy of (the Name) 'Beginningless'? How should that which does not transcend being produced (*inshā'*) produce the things (of the world)? There then would have arisen in Him a sign of having been made (*al-maṣnūᶜ*) and He would become a proof (*dalīl*) after having been the proven (*madlūl ᶜalayh*).[121]

"There is no argument in absurd opinions (such as the above), no answer when it (absurdity) is asked about, no glorification of Him in its meaning.[122] Nor is there any ill in distinguishing Him from creation, unless it be that the Eternal accepts not to be made two, nor the Beginningless to have a beginning.[123]

"There is no god but God, the All-high, the Tremendous. They have cried lies who ascribe equals to God! They have gone astray into far error and suffered a manifest loss![124] And God bless Muhammad and his household, the pure."

2. *The Veil*

It was related from Muḥammad ibn 'Abdallāh al-Khurāsānī, the servant of al-Riḍā — upon whom be peace — that a man from among the unbelievers (*zanādiqah*)[125] entered the presence of the Imam, with whom was a group of people. Abu-l-Ḥasan (the Imam) said to him,

"Dost thou see that if the correct view is your view — and it is not your view — then are we not equal? All that we have prayed, fasted, given of the alms and declared of our convictions will not harm us."

The unbeliever remained silent. Then Abu-l-Ḥasan said, "If the correct view is our view — and it is our view — then have not you perished and we gained salvation?"

He said, "God's mercy be upon thee. Then let me know, how is He and where is He?"

Abu-l-Ḥasan answered, "Woe upon thee, surely the opinion thou hast adopted is mistaken. He determined the 'where', and He was, when there was no where; and He fashioned the 'how', and He was, when there was no 'how'. So He is not known through 'howness' or 'whereness' or through any form of sense perception, nor can He be gauged by anything."

The man said, "So then surely He is nothing (*lā shay'*) if He cannot be perceived by any of the senses."

Abu-l-Ḥasan said, "Woe upon thee! When thy senses fail to perceive Him, thou deniest His lordship. But when our senses fail to perceive Him, we know for certain that He is our Lord and that He is something different from other things (*shay' bi-khilāf al-ashyā'*)."[126]

The man said, "Then tell me, when was He?"

Abu-l-Ḥasan said, "Tell when He was not, and then I will tell you when He was."[127]

The man said, "Then what is the proof of Him?"

Abu-l-Ḥasan said, "Surely when I contemplate my body and it is impossible for me to increase or decrease its breadth and height, or to keep unpleasent things away from it or draw benefits to it, then I know that this structure has a maker and I acknowledge (*iqrār*) Him — even though that which I had seen of the rotation of the celestial sphere through His power; the producing of clouds;[128] the turning about of the winds;[129] the procession of the sun, the moon and the stars; and others of His wondrous and perfectly created signs (*āyāt*), had (already) made me know that (all) this has a Determiner (*muqaddir*) and Producer (*munshi'*)."

The man said, "Then why has He veiled Himself (from men)?"

Abu-l-Ḥasan replied, "Surely the veil is upon creatures because of the abundance of their sins. As for Him, no secret is hidden from Him during the day or the night."[130]

The man said, "Then why does the sense of sight perceive Him not?"

Abu-l-Ḥasan answered, "Because of the difference between Him and His creatures, who are perceived by the vision of the eyes, whether their own or others. Then He is greater than that sight should perceive Him, imagination encompass Him, or the power of reason delineate Him."

The man said, "Then define His limits (*ḥadd*) for me."

He answered, "He has no limits."

The man asked, "Why?"

He answered, "Because every limited thing (*maḥdūd*) ends at a limit. If limitation (*taḥdīd*) is possible, then increase is possible. If increase is possible, then decrease is possible. So He is unlimited. He neither increases nor decreases. Nor is He capable of being divided or imagined."

The man said, "Then tell me about your saying that He is Subtle, Hearing, Seeing, Knowing and Wise.[131] Can He be the Hearing without ears, the Seeing without eyes, the Subtle without working with the hands and the Wise without workmanship (*ṣanʿah*)?"[132]

Abu-l-Ḥasan said, "Surely a person among us is subtle in accordance with (his) skill in workmanship. Hast thou not seen the man who undertakes a task and is subtle in his handling of it, so that it is said, 'How subtle is so and so!' Then how should it not be said of the Majestic Creator that He is Subtle, when He creates a subtle and majestic[133] creation, places in its living creatures their souls, creates every kind different in form from its own kind, and none resembles another? Each possesses in the composition of its form a subtlety from the Subtle and Aware Creator.

"Then we looked upon the trees and their bearing of delicate things, whether edible or inedible, and we said at that, 'Surely our Creator is Subtle, (but) not like the subtlety of His creatures in their workmanship.' And we said, 'Surely He is Hearing, for not hidden from Him are the sounds of His creatures between the Throne and the earth, from a mote to what is larger than it, and in the land and the sea. And their words are not confused by Him.' At that we said, 'Surely He is Hearing, but not through ears.'

"Then we said, 'Surely He is Seeing, but not through eyes, for He sees the trace of a black speck on a dark night on a black stone.[134] He sees the tracks of an ant on a pitch-black night. He sees what is harmful for it and what beneficial, and the result of its cohabitation, and its young and descendents.' And at that we said, 'Surely He is Seeing, but not like the sight of His creatures'."

The man did not leave until he had embraced Islam. The Imam said other things as well.

NOTES

1 The Prophet said, "The number of paths to God is equal to the number of human souls."

2 Throughout these texts, as in all traditional Muslim writings, whenever the name of the Prophet or a pronoun referring to him is mentioned, phrases like "Upon whom be blessings and peace" are added. In the same way for the Imams "Upon whom be peace" is added. For the most part these phrases have been dropped in translation.

3 According to Majlisī the meaning is that God's exaltation, magnificence and divinity are not dependent upon creation, but existed before it (p. 288). I.e., although these terms logically imply duality (exalted in relation to the debased, divine in relation to creatures, etc.), they express qualities which God possessed in His eternal nature "before" any creature existed. The same can be said about His solitariness.

4 Cf. Quran XXI, 30: "The heavens and the earth were a mass all sewn up, and then we unstitched them."

5 Reference to Quran VI, 97: "He splits the sky into dawn".

6 Chapter and verse of Quranic quotations will be indicated in the text in this manner. I have relied largely on the Arberry and Pickthall translations.

7 Cf. for example Quran XIV, 44: "And warn mankind of the day when the chastisement comes on them, and those who did evil shall say, 'Our Lord, defer us to a near term, and we will answer Thy call, and follow the Messengers'."

8 Majlisī offers several explanations for this passage, and he comments as follows on the interpretation followed here: "He wished that creatures profess His Unity alone, without associating any others with Him. For if He were apparent to minds and the senses, He would be associated with possible beings in unreal unity (*al-waḥdat al-iᶜtibāriyyah*). Then the unity which pertained to Him would not belong to Him alone" (p. 289).

9 Cf. Quran IV, 165: "Messengers bearing good tidings, and warning, so that mankind might have no argument against God, after the Messengers"; and VI, 150: "To God belongs the argument conclusive."

10 Cf. for example, Quran XXII, 78: "That the Messenger might be a witness against you . . . ."

11 "Similarity" or "comparison" (*tashbih*) becomes an important technical term in Islamic theology and Sufism. It indicates the belief that God's attributes can be likened to those of man and the creatures. Hence scholars have often translated the term as "anthropomorphism". It is contrasted with "incompara-
Heaven, which are mentioned in several Quranic verses, such as the following:

bility" (*tanzih*), the belief that God's attributes are in no way similar to those of the creatures. As pointed out in the introduction, the Imams emphasize the latter position throughout these texts, without failing to make use of the former to explain their points. In later theology and Sufism, attempts are often made to strike a balance between the two positions by maintaining that God is neither completely similar to His creatures nor totally incomparable, or that He is both similar and incomparable at the same time. For example, Ibn al-ᶜArabī attempts to strike this balance in the third chapter of his celebrated *Fuṣūṣ al-ḥikam*. See W. Chittick, "Ibn ᶜArabī's own Summary of the *Fuṣūṣ*: 'The Imprint of the Bezels of Wisdom'," *Sophia Perennis*, vol. 1, no. 2, Autumn 1975, pp. 108-110.

12 As pointed out by Majlisī (pp. 223-4), this is "a rejection of the views of those who say that every temporal being (*ḥādith*) must come from a (pre-existing) matter (*māddah*)."

13 The words *ayniyyah*, *kayfiyyah* and *ḥaythiyyah* could be translated more literally as "whereness", "howness" and "whereasness" (cf. above, p.26, and below, p. 49). Majlisī explains the meaning as follows: "In other words, He is not localized in any one place that He should be in that place without being in another, as is the case with things qualified by localization (*mutamakkināt*). So He cannot be perceived like something possessing location and place. The relation of a disengaged reality (*mujarrad*) to all places is equal. No place is empty of Him in respect of the fact He encompasses them in knowledge, in terms of causality, and because He preserves and sustains them .....

"There is no object like Him existing either externally (*fi'-l-khārij*) or mentally (*fi'-l-adhhān*), that He might be described as possessing any of the various qualities relating to corporeality and possibility. It is also possible that by 'quality' is meant 'cognitive form' (*al-ṣūrat al-ᶜilmiyyah*).

"And He is not absent from anything, that is, ... in respect of knowledge, that one might thus conclude that He possesses aspect (*ḥayth*) and place (*makān*). As for things qualified by place, it is in their nature to be absent from (other) things and not to encompass them in knowledge. This sentence is as if to emphasize the former statement. It is also possible that 'aspect' here refers to time ..." (p. 224).

14 "The changing essences of things make Him inaccessible to minds ... either because, if the mind could perceive Him, He would be — like possible beings — a locus for changing attributes, and thus He would be in need of a maker; or because reason tells us that the Maker must be different in attribute from the made, so He cannot be perceived as are created things ..." (Majlisī, p. 225).

15 Cf. Quran XVIII, 110: "Say, 'If the sea were ink for the Words of my Lord, the sea would be spent before the Words of my Lord are spent, though We brought replenishment the like of it."

16 It will not have passed unnoticed that the transcendence of the divine Essence is emphasized here by the fact that man is dumbfounded even by the lower reaches of God's theophanies. The powers of man's reason are stopped by the waves, they do not reach the current itself. The mere mention of God's eternity bewilders the imagination, etc.

17 According to Majlisī the reference is to the "cords" (*asbāb*) or degrees of

"Pharoah said, 'Haman, build for me a tower, that haply so I may reach the cords, the cords of the heavens, and look upon Moses' God' " (XL, 36-7).

18 The same words, *itqān al-ṣunᶜ*, are used together once in the Quran: "God's handiwork, who has made everything perfectly" (XXVII, 88).

19 The fact that the creation displays the signs and portents of God is of course emphasized throughout the Quran and all of Islam and is the basis of all Islamic cosmology. For the Muslim, moreover, it is the very order and regularity of the universe and nature's laws which prove God. See S. H. Nasr, *Science and Civilization in Islam*, Cambridge (Mass.), 1968.

20 According to Majlisī by "tree" is meant first the Abrahamic line of prophecy, then the tribe and family of the Prophet — the Quraysh and Banū Hāshim (p. 227). The descriptions following all refer to the tree of prophecy and the prophets who grew from it.

21 I.e., Gabriel, the angel of revelation. Cf. Quran XXVI, 192-3: "Truly it is the revelation of the Lord of all beings, brought down by the Faithful Spirit . . ."

22 I.e., revelation.

23 The Quran.

24 The "steed" which carried the Prophet to Heaven on his night journey (*miᶜrāj*).

25 I.e., during the Prophet's *miᶜrāj*.

26 Cf. Quran XV, 94: "So proclaim that which thou art commanded, and withdraw from the idolators."

27 Cf. Quran V, 67: "O Messenger, deliver that which has been sent down to thee from thy Lord . . ."

28 According to a *ḥadīth* of the Prophet, "I cannot enumerate all of Thy praises: Thou art as Thou hast praised Thyself".

29 Cf. Quran XIV, 34 and XVI, 18.

30 Cf. Quran XVII, 51: "Then they will say, 'Who will bring us back?' Say: 'He who originated you the first time'."

31 Cf. Quran XXX, 46: "And of His signs is that He looses the winds, bearing good tidings and that He may let you taste of His mercy", and other similar verses.

32 Cf. Quran XVI, 15: "And He cast on the earth firm mountains, lest it shake with you"; also XXI, 31 and XXXI, 10.

33 The editor comments as follows in a footnote: "The perfection of professing His Unity is to maintain that He is not forced to act as He does and is devoid of all faults, to declare Him to be above the blemishes of incapacity and imperfection, and to profess that He is pure of what pertains to and impinges upon possible beings, such as corporeality, composition, and other negative (*salbī*) attributes" (p. 251). Sincerity is to profess the Unity of God in a perfect manner, so that eventually at the end of the path of spiritual realization and perfection (*al-ṭarīqah*), all stains of contingency are removed both from the knowledge and the being of the believer.

34 This sentence does not occur in the *Biḥār al-anwār*, but it does occur in the same passage in the *Nahj al-balāghah* and seems necessary from the context.

35 I.e., to their "appointed terms" to use Quranic language (III, 145, etc.). The text of the *Nahj al-balāghah* reads "*aḥāl*" for "*ajjal*", which would change

the translation to the following: "He transforms things at their (proper) times."

36 "The relation (of this image) to the saying that minerals are generated from the vapors of the earth is obvious" (Majlisī, p. 278).

37 On the Islamic teaching that the angels, though of luminous substance, are "peripheral" beings since they know only some of God's Names, while man is "central" since he knows all of His Names, see F. Schuon, *The Transcendent Unity of Religions*, London, 1953, pp. 70-72.

38 "Reason's powers" is a translation of *ᶜuqūl*, plural of *ᶜaql*. A more awkward but perhaps more exact translation would be "reasons". Many scholars translate the word *ᶜaql* as "intellect" or "intelligence". Certainly all of these translations are possible, since the various meanings are all contained in the one Arabic word — if indeed the reader will concede that there is more than one basic meaning, for in modern thought the distinction between the reason (*ratio*) and the intellect (*intellectus*) has largely been ignored.

However that may be, the Arabic word *ᶜaql* may be said to possess at least two significations according to various contexts. It may signify the Universal Intellect, which is equivalent to the Greatest Spirit and the Muhammadan Light. It is God's first creation and possesses true and detailed knowledge of all things, including God Himself. It may also signify the "reason", which is the reflection of the Universal Intellect upon the human plane. But in ordinary men the reason is cut off from the Intellect. Only the prophets and saints may be said to have actualized their "intellects" to various degrees. In other words, they have realized an inward identity with the Universal Intellect.

But in these texts, the Imams usually speak of *ᶜaql* as cut off from its luminous and spiritual source. It limits and constricts the infinite Truth in keeping with its root meaning (*ᶜaqala* = to tie, to bind). Hence I translate the word as "reason" or "power of reason". When the Imams speak of the actualization of the intellect within man, they refer to the "heart" (*qalb*). The reason cannot understand God, but, as we shall see below, the heart may see Him. Most Sufis follow this terminology, such as the members of Ibn al-ᶜArabī's school (see my forthcoming study of Ṣadr al-Dīn al-Qūnawī). But all are aware of the *ᶜaql's* dual nature. Thus Rūmī: "The particular intellect (*ᶜaql-i juzwī* — reason) has disgraced the Intellect" (*Mathnawī*, V, 463).

Nevertheless, the Imams do not ignore the positive role that *ᶜaql* — and here perhaps "intelligence" would be the best translation — can and does play in religion, in keeping with Islam's fundamental emphasis upon knowledge (see F. Rosenthal, *Knowledge Triumphant*, Leiden, 1970). The first book of the section on *uṣūl* from al-Kulaynī's *al-Kāfī* is entitled the "Book of *ᶜAql*." It contains such *ḥadiths* as the following: "The intelligence is that through which man worships the All-Merciful and gains Paradise" (Imam Jaᶜfar). "The sincere friend of every man is his intelligence, while his enemy is his ignorance" (Imam ᶜAlī al-Riḍā). "He who possesses intelligence possesses religion, and he who possesses religion enters the Garden" (Imam Jaᶜfar). "In the reckoning on the Day of Resurrection God will only scrutinize His servants to the extent He has given them intelligence in the world" (Imam Mūsā). The first selection from Imam ᶜAl-Riḍā below (pp. 44-48) refers in several places to the positive function of the *ᶜaql*.

The two roles of the *ᶜaql* to which the Imams allude, positive and negative, derive from the principle enunciated by the Prophet in the *ḥadith:* "Meditate upon God's bounties, but not upon His Essence." The *ᶜaql* must be able to see that the world by its very nature manifests a Reality beyond it. A healthy intelligence, one which on the human plane reflects the First Intellect directly, will naturally see the signs of God in all things. But as soon as the *ᶜaql* tries to understand the very Essence of God, it oversteps its boundaries and goes astray.

39 Majlisī interprets the "deviation of straying" to mean the "reason, whose nature is deviation and straying" (p. 281).

40 This divine Name occurs several times in the Quran, such as XL, 15.

41 As the Quran often affirms, both explicitly and implicitly, "He directs the affair" (XIII, 2, etc.).

42 Cf. Quran II, 148: "Every man has his direction to which he turns." Majlisī cites the *ḥadīth,* "All are eased to what has been created for them", which in turn recalls Quran LXXX, 19-21: "He created him (man), and determined him, then the way eased for him . . .".

43 Both the editor in a footnote, pointing to the printed edition of *al-Tawḥīd,* and Majlisī in his commentary, basing himself on a similar passage in the *Nahj al-balāghah,* suggest that the correct reading is *ḥudūd* for *maḥdūd.* The translation has been made accordingly.

44 Cf. Quran L, 38: "We created the heavens and the earth, and what between them is, in six days, and no weariness touched us."

45 The commentator points out that *mukābadah* occurs in place of *mukāyadah* in some manuscripts, which would change the translation of the last clause to the following: "or from hardship from one who would transgress His command" (p. 280).

46 According to a footnote to the text another manuscript reads "when He" for "and".

47 These are the words of the people who were led astray by the followers of Iblīs disputing with them in hell. The verse continues: "It was naught but the sinners that led us astray; so we have no intercessors, no loyal friend. O that we might return again, and be among the believers!"

48 Passages of the Quran known as "clear" (*muḥkam*) are those about whose meaning there can be no question. They are contrasted with other passages known as "ambiguous" (*mutashābih*), which are open to various interpretations, even in the outward and literal meaning of the text.

49 The commentator remarks: "The subtlety of the comparison of reflection, or the mind, where reflection takes place, to a bird's craw will not be lost on the reader" (p. 284).

50 Cf. Quran II, 231: "And remember God's blessing upon you, and the Book and the Wisdom He has sent down on you . . ."; and II, 269: "Whoso is given the Wisdom, has been given much good."

51 A term appearing twice in the Quran (III, 7 and IV, 162). In Sufism and Shi'ism it is usually taken to refer to those who, due to their elevated spiritual station, are qualified to speak of the divine mysteries.

52 The son of ᶜAlī's sister, Umm Hānī bint Abī Ṭālib. For the scant bibliographical references see *Biḥār al-anwār,* vol. 4, p. 313 and the *Lughat-nāmah* of Dihkhudā (Tehran, 1325/1946 onward).

53 A reference to much prostration in prayer. Cf. Quran XLVIII, 29: "Their

mark is on their face, the trace of prostration."

54 The Quran emphasises that "To God is the homecoming" (XXXV, 18; cf. also II, 285; III, 28, etc). Likewise, "Unto God belongs the issue of all affairs" is a Quranic expression (XXII, 41; XXXI, 22).

55 Cf. Quran XLII, 26: "And He answers those who believe and do righteous deeds, and gives them increase of His bounty."

56 Reference to Quran I, 4: "To Thee alone we pray for succour."

57 "God is He who raised up the heavens without pillars you can see..." (Quran XIII, 2; cf. XXXI, 10).

58 A reference to their creation: "The only words We say to a thing, when We desire it, is that We say to it 'Be', and it is" (Quran XVI, 40).

59 A reference to Quran XXXV, 10: "To Him good words go up, and the righteous deed — He uplifts it."

60 Literally, "the neighboring dark-reds", i.e., as explained by Muḥammad ᶜAbduh in his commentary on the *Nahj al-balāghah* (vol. II, p. 126), a reference to the mountains in terms of their color from afar.

61 Majlisī remarks, "If you say, 'He — glory be to Him — knows what the lightning illumines and what it does not illumine, so why should the Imam specify what the lightning vanishes from?' I would answer, 'Because His knowledge of what is not illumined is stranger and more wonderful. Since, as for what is illumined by the lightning, it is possible that anyone of correct vision would also know it" (p. 316).

62 A reference to ancient Arabian beliefs concerning the influence of the moon in its various mansions on the weather. See the article "Anwā'" in the *Encyclopaedia of Islam* (new edition), vol. 1, pp. 523-4.

63 Cf. Quran II, 26: "God is not ashamed to strike a similitude even of a gnat".

64 "God knows what every female bears" (Quran XIII, 8).

65 Since He already knows their needs, or since He is the "All-Hearing" in His Essence.

66 Majlisī comments: He is not described by pairs, "i.e. by likes, or by opposites; or by the attributes of pairs; or there is no composition in Him as the result of the marriage of any two things..." (p. 316).

67 *ᶜIlāj*. If He did, it would suggest that there is something upon which He works or to which He applies Himself. Rather, "He but says to it 'Be', and it is" (Quran II, 117; III, 47, etc.).

68 See Quran IV, 164.

69 Cf. Quran XX, 23.

70 Literally, "uvulae", *lahawāt*.

71 A divine Name occurring in Quran XXIII, 14 and XXXVII, 125.

72 The famous Battle of the Camel occurred in the year 36/656 between the followers of ᶜAlī and those of Ṭalḥah and Zubayr. See the *Encyclopaedia of Islam* (new edition), "Djamal", vol. II, pp. 414-16.

73 This is a reference to the Quranic verse, "They are unbelievers who say, 'God is the Third of Three'" (V, 73). Concerning the providential Quranic "misunderstanding" of the Christian Trinity, see F. Schuon, *The Transcendent Unity of Religions*, pp. 40 ff.

74 The first kind of "unity" that is rejected is numerical unity, or the idea

that when we say "He is one God", we mean something similar to what we mean when we say, "This is one walnut", i.e., that there may also be two Gods, three Gods, etc. The second "unity" refers to similarity in kind or species, as when we say, "This is one cat", meaning that there are also other kinds of cats. In the words of Majlisī, "When it is said in this sense of a Byzantine that he is one of mankind, it is meant that his kind is one of the kinds of men or is a kind among other kinds" (p. 207). This is *tashbih* because we are comparing God to whatever we say He is one of. Since He is one of that kind, He has to be similar to others of that kind.

75 As Majlisī points out, the first of the acceptable meanings of divine Unity is that He is one in the sense that He has no second, associate or partner. Only He truly *is*. And the second is that He has no parts in any sense whatsoever (p. 207).

76 The discrepancies between the present translation of this passage and that found in *Shi'ite Islam*, p. 127, are due to the fact that in *Shi'ite Islam* the passage has been translated from ʿAllāmah Ṭabāṭabā'ī's Persian translation, which includes his commentary.

77 God's signs are displayed through the whole of creation, as indicated in many passages of the Quran, as for example, in the verse "In the alternation of night and day, and what God has created in the heavens and the earth — surely there are signs for a godfearing people" (X, 6).

78 The translation of this sentence follows the first interpretation offered by the commentator. According to the second, which seems less likely in the context, *wujūd* would mean "existence" as it usually does in current usage, and the meaning would be: "His existence (being manifestly evident) necessitates affirming Him (i.e. attesting to Him)".

79 The editor notes that in the printed edition of *al-Tawḥīd* the text reads, "So it is not said that anything is after Him."

80 As in many similar sayings of the Imams, the purpose of this passage is to affirm both God's "similarity" to creatures and His "incomparability" with them by stating that His attributes must not be understood in the usual sense of the words. Normally if we say "outward", we mean that which is immediately perceptible to the senses, but God's "outwardness" is of a different kind. Majlisī comments in detail upon this passage. Here we can quote his remarks on some of the less obvious clauses: "Inward, i.e. not in terms of spatial distance, in the sense that He would move from one place to another in order to become hidden, or that He would enter into creatures' inner parts in order to know them. Rather, in His inmost center He is hidden from the powers of man's reason, and He knows his inner parts and his secrets .... His nearness is not the spatial nearness acquired by approaching things, but derives from knowledge, His causal relationship to the creatures, His originating growth and development within them, and His mercy (which encompasses them). He is Subtle not by being a body with a delicate constitution, small volume, strange and wondrous structure, or in that He is colorless, but by creating subtle things and knowing them; or by His incorporeality and 'disengagement' (*tajarrud*). 'Not through coercion', that is, He is free and not forced in His activity .... 'Not through the activity of thought': in other words, when He determines things He does not need the flow or activity of thought" (pp. 236-7).

81 Reference to Quran II, 255.

82 Majlisī comments: "When He creates sense organs and bestows them upon the creatures, it is known that He has no sense organs. This is either because of what has already been said about the fact that He does not possess the attributes of creatures; or because, when we see that He has bestowed sense organs, we become aware that we need them in order to perceive. Then we conclude that He transcends them, since it is impossible for Him to be in need of anything. It may also be because the reason judges that He differs from His creatures in attributes" (pp. 237-8). Majlisī also quotes (pp. 238-9) a long philosophical and metaphysical discussion of this sentence by Ibn Maytham, one of the commentators of the *Nahj al-balāghah.*

83 "In other words, since their realities have become actualized and their quiddities have been brought into existence, it is known that they are possible beings. Now every possible being needs an origin. The Origin of origins will not be one of these realities (which have become externally actualized)" (Majlisī, p. 239).

84 "When we see that He created opposites and that they need a particular situation or position to manifest themselves, we realize that He is not opposite to anything, for to need something contradicts the Necessity (*wujūb*) of Being. Or the meaning is that when we see that each one of two opposite things prevents, repels and negates the existence of the other, we realize that He transcends that. Or we see that opposition occurs through delimitation by certain limits which are unable to embrace other limits, as for example (in the case of) different colors or qualities, while He transcends all limits. In the same way, how should the Creator oppose His creatures, or He who causes to issue forth (*al-fā'iḍ*) oppose that which is issued forth (*al-mafīḍ*)? Or if we understand opposite to mean that which is equal in strength, this would necessitate another Necessary Being, the impossibility of which has already been proven" (Majlisī, p. 239).

85 In a footnote the editor mentions that some copies of *ᶜUyūn akhbār al-Riḍā*, one of the sources of this passage, read *al-jaff* (dryness) for *al-jasū* (solidity).

86 The Ascending Stairways (*al-maᶜārij*) are mentioned in the Quran, LXX, 3. The meaning would seem to be that at death, if the spirit of one who has compared things to his Lord tries to ascend towards Him, it is blinded by His power. Compare Rūmī: "Make it thy habit to behold the Light without the glass, in order that when the glass is shattered there may not be blindness (in thee)" (*Mathnawī*, V, 991).

87 The text reads "it" for "dominion", but in order to avoid ambiguity the noun has been repeated. In Arabic the masculine pronoun cannot refer to the feminine "power", although if one were to follow the similar sentence in the *ḥadīth* related from the Seventh Imam below, "power" would be the logical choice as antecedent. The meaning is that before the production of the world God had power over it, and after its end He will still possess it. Whether or not it exists in external form is irrelevant.

88 Cf. Quran LII, 45: "Then leave them, till they encounter their day wherein they shall be thunderstruck . . .".

89 Cf. Quran XXI, 23: "He shall not be questioned as to what He does, but they shall be questioned."

90 *Lā yaqaᶜ ᶜalā shay'*. The meaning is not completely clear. The editor points

out in a footnote (p. 300) that in the *Uṣūl min al-kāfī* the text of this *ḥadīth* reads *yandam* for *yaqa*ᶜ, i.e., "He becomes remorseful at nothing."

91 This verse is in reference to the covenant made between God and man before the creation of the world. See S. H. Nasr, *Ideals and Realities of Islam*, London, 1966, pp. 25-7.

92 God is often referred to as a "thing" (*shay'*) in the *ḥadīth* literature, as well as in theology and philosophy, since the meaning of the word "thing" in Arabic is not limited to external, concrete existents. Rather, it signifies reality, entity or quiddity, at whatever level of existence, from the most sublime to the most concrete.

93 Majlisī interprets this to mean the "script written by hands" (p. 162). I.e., neither the spoken nor the written name is the Named.

94 The meaning of this sentence is obscure in the Arabic and Majlisī offers at least eight possible readings (pp. 162-3), some of which are very close to one another, and the most likely of which has been followed here. The present interpretation is also that offered by the editor of *al-Tawḥīd*, p. 58.

95 Majlisī comments that this sentence has been interpreted to mean that "God has not come into being. If He had, He would have been originated by another, and His Being as well as the attributes of His origination would be known by means of the fashioning of His maker, just as effects are known by their causes." But, he adds, "In my view perhaps the meaning is that He has not been fashioned and that therefore He cannot be known by comparing Him to something else which has been fashioned" (p. 163). According to this interpretation, the sentence should be translated as follows: "He has not come into being that His Being should be known through something else which has been fashioned."

96 Majlisī comments: "Between the Creator and His creatures there is no common matter (*māddah*) or reality (*ḥaqīqah*) which might allow them to attain to knowledge of Him; rather, He produced them from nothing that was" (p. 165). This passage may also be interpreted to mean, in accordance with the beginning of the paragraph, "There is nothing to act as a veil between the Creator and His creatures."

97 This passage is related up to this point in the *Uṣūl min al-kāfī*. The Tehran edition of 1388/1968-9, published with a Persian translation and notes by one of the well-known contemporary ᶜ*ulamā'*, Āyatallāh Muḥammad Bāqir Kamara'ī, contains the following commentary (vol. I, pp. 207-8): "The Names of God are His theophanies (*jilwah-hā*) which cast a ray of light upon man's reason (*khirad*). Because they become connected to human reason, limit, end and definition (*ghāyah*, *nihāyah*, *ḥadd*) apply to them. The limit of each being lies where it is connected to another being. The theophanies of God's act (*fi*ᶜ*l*) and fashioning (*ṣan*ᶜ*ah*), which are His creation, become limited in the framework of possible beings (*mumkināt*). There the ray of light which brings about creation comes to its limit. Thus is is said, 'the existence of a man', or 'of a tree', 'of an angel', 'of the earth', 'of heaven', etc.

"The theophanies of God's attributes (*ṣifāt*), which are the principle (*mabda'*) of the theophanies of (His) act, are given limits by the functioning of the reason, and thus it is said, God's 'knowledge', 'power', and 'life'. In this way the Names become distinct from the divine Essence, and even the all-inclusive (*jāmi*ᶜ) Name of God, which is 'Allah', is separated from the Essence. The reality of God is other than all of these."

98 *Maᶜrifah* within the essentially gnostic perspective of Islam is the goal of religious endeavour. See F. Schuon, *Understanding Islam*, London, 1962, chapter 1. As explained in the following footnote, the meaning of this sentence is that man has faith not in something which he himself does not know, but in that upon which all of his knowledge is based and which is in fact the object of all knowledge. To the extent he has knowledge, he has knowledge of God, albeit imperfectly, since there is no other knowledge.

99 In an unpublished work entitled *Risālat al-walāyah* (*Treatise on sanctity*), ᶜAllāmah Ṭabāṭabā'ī comments on the section of this passage beginning with the words "Whoso maintains that he knows God by means of a veil": "Allusion is made here to the fact that it is logically impossible for the knowledge of something other than God to make necessary the knowledge of God Himself. Because of God's transcendence, it cannot be said that knowledge (of Him) is the very same as the thing known, as has already been explained (earlier in the treatise).

"It is impossible that knowledge of one thing should be knowledge of another thing different from it: otherwise the two different things would be the same, which contradicts the premise. So the fact that knowledge of one thing renders the knowledge of another thing necessary requires some sort of unification (*ittiḥād*) between the two things. But since they have been postulated as two things, there must be in addition to an aspect of unification, an aspect of disparity. Thus each of them is compounded of two aspects. Whereas God — glory be to Him — is one and simple in essence: He is not compounded of anything in a manner which would allow Him to be known by other than Him. This point is indicated by the Imam's saying, 'There is nothing between the Creator and the created,' etc., as well as by his words, 'Then he who maintains that he has faith in that which he does not know has gone astray from knowledge', etc., which is derived from his previous saying, i.e., 'Surely he alone knows God who knows Him by means of God,' etc. His words, 'A created thing perceives nothing unless it be by means of God', serve as its proof, for everything is known by means of God, who is 'the Light of the heavens and the earth' (Quran XXIV, 35); so how should things be known by means of other than Him? For He supports every individual being (*dhāt*), and He is without supports in His very Essence (*dhāt*). At the same time, knowledge of that which in its very essence is dependent ensues from knowledge of the Independent Being which supports it, for the fact that knowledge takes form necessarily requires independence in the case of that which is known. Thus knowledge of what is dependent is a consequence of (knowledge of) the Independent which accompanies it. Such is the reality.

"And since it might be imagined that this doctrine is incarnation (*ḥulūl*) or unification (*ittiḥād*) — high be God exalted above these — the Imam follows his words by saying, 'God is empty of His creatures and His creatures are empty of Him', etc. Saying that the created being's perception of something is by means of God does not negate the beginning of the passage ('Whoso asserts . . .'), which denies that the knowledge of God should require knowledge of other than Him, for the knowledge which is spoken of at the beginning is acquired (*ḥuṣūlī*, i.e., rational), and that at the end is 'presential' (*ḥuḍūrī*, i.e., direct and divinely dispensed knowledge or gnosis)." Folio 26 obverse-reverse (Photocopies of this work are in the possession of a number of ᶜAllāmah Ṭabāṭabā'ī's disciples and students, and it is hoped that some day it will be published).

100 In *al-Tawḥīd* the editor explains that here the second *makān* is equivalent to *makānah* or *aẓamah*. He comments, "He did not create a place for His station and grandeur because places encompass Him not" (p. 141). Majlisī prefers the reading *kān* for *makān* as found in some manuscripts and also in the *ḥadīth* from the fifth Imam translated above. The meaning would then be as translated there, i.e., "He did not bring into existence a place for His Being."

101 "Master of the dominion" (*mālik al-mulk*) is a divine name, occurring in Quran III, 26. Cf. Quran III, 189: "To God belongs the dominion of the heavens and the earth: and God is powerful over everything" and many similar verses.

102 Cf. Quran, LII, 45.

103 The famous Abbasid caliph, son of Hārūn al-Rashīd. On his decision to appoint Imam al-Riḍā as his successor, see *Shīᶜite Islam*.

104 In general Banū Hāshim ("The sons of Hāshim") have been understood to be the descendents of Hāshim ibn ᶜAbd Manāf, the great grandfather of the Prophet and also the ancestor of ᶜAlī and al-ᶜAbbās, half-brother of the Prophet's father, from whom is taken the name of the Abbasid caliphate. During the Abbasid period the term refers to the family of the Prophet, but more specifically, as here, to the Abbasid family itself. See B. Lewis, "Hāshimiyyah", *The Encyclopedia of Islam* (new edition), vol. III, p. 265.

105 Majlisī offers four possible explanations for this sentence, the simplest of which is as follows: "Everything whose existence can be known immediately through the senses without inference from its effects is fashioned (since it is a part of the created world)" (p. 233).

106 Men are not separated from God because they are in one place and He in another, but because He is free of place and localization, whereas they are entrapped within it (Majlisī, p. 233).

107 Majlisī comments: " 'His names are an expression', or they are not His very Essence and Attributes, rather they are means of expressing and speaking of them. 'And His acts are to make understood', so that men will come to know Him through them and they will infer His existence, knowledge, power, wisdom and mercy. 'And His Essence is Reality', or a hidden, transcendent reality not reached by the powers of the creatures' reason" (p. 234).

108 Majlisī offers several interpretations for this passage. According to the one which is largely followed here, "To associate an end with Him . . . means to come to the conclusion that He undergoes annihilation along with the creatures, so that it would be correct to say, 'His end is before, or after, the end of so and so.' This is the same as to say that He participates wholly in the nature of creatures and therefore has parts. Whoso says this has described Him as possessing possibility, incapacity and the other defects of possible beings. And whoso judges such has deviated concerning the divine Essence" (p. 235).

109 From this sentence begins a long section which corresponds almost exactly with the *ḥadīth* quoted from Imam ᶜAlī above (pp. 38 ff). For this reason the original Arabic terms have not been repeated. It might be tempting to take this

correspondence as proof that the attribution of these words to ᶜAlī al-Riḍā or to ᶜAlī is incorrect. But one must remember that it is quite common for the Imams to quote their fathers and grandfathers, all the way back to the Prophet. We have seen examples of this already in the chain of authority of a number of *ḥadiths* translated above. Moreover, in the middle of a discourse there is no particular reason for the Imam to stop and point out exactly whom he is quoting, just as is the case with quotations from the Quran, especially since most of his followers would know perfectly well. The traditional explanation for the repetition is summed up by Shaykh al-Ṣadūq (*al-Tawḥīd*, p. 309; see also Majlisī, p. 306): "In the *ḥadīth* of ᶜAlī there are certain words which Imam Riḍā mentioned in his sermon. This is a confirmation of what we have always said concerning the Imams, upon whom be peace: the knowledge of each of them is derived from his father right back to the Prophet."

110 This and the previous phrase are essentially the same in meaning. Normally, when man wills or desires to do something, he has a particular idea or goal and then exerts himself to achieve it, employing resolution and diligence. But as for God, "His command, when He desires a thing, is to say to it 'Be', and it is" (Quran XXXVI, 82).

111 *Qad* often cannot be translated by a separate word in English. It indicates the termination of action at the moment of speaking and therefore as Majlisī notes, quoting the classical grammarians, serves "to approximate the past to the present" (p. 242).

112 Majlisī explains that none of these words can refer to God since each of them implies temporal or other limitation, while God transcends time and knows all things in eternity. Thus, "ever since" indicates a point of beginning in time, and if it applied to God it would indicate that what was before that point was concealed from Him. He can have no doubts concerning the future, so "perhaps" cannot apply to Him, etc. (pp. 241-2).

113 Majlisī remarks that "instruments and means . . . or physical organs and corporeal faculties . . . allude to the existence of corporeality like themselves . . . And it is not improbable that by 'instruments' are meant the words which are negated from Him in the previous section and that this passage is meant to be an explanation of that" (p. 242).

114 "The activities and the results of these instruments and means are found in creatures, not in God" (Majlisī, p. 242).

115 "The fact that the words *mudh*, *qad* and *law lā* are attributed to instruments indicate that the latter are neither beginningless, nor eternal, nor perfect. Therefore instruments could not delimit or allude to Him because, by reason of their temporality and imperfection, they are far from being commensurate with (God,) the Perfect, Absolute and Eternal in His Essence . . . (This is) because *mudh* refers to beginning in time . . . *qad* approximates the past to the present . . . and *law lā* is employed to speak of what would have been good . . . (for example), 'How good it would have been *if only* it had been such and such' . . . and thus it points to imperfection in the situation and deters from absolute perfection" (Majlisī, p. 243). Majlisī also points out two alternative readings for this passage which need not concern us here.

116 The text reads "through them", and in a long passage (pp. 242-3) Majlisī demonstrates that the pronoun should refer to "powers of reason" rather than

to "instruments", although in a similar passage in the *Nahj al-balāghah* it refers to the latter.

117 "He becomes veiled to sight through the powers of reason because it is the powers of reason which judge that the vision of Him is impossible, and it is to the powers of reason that imaginations appeal when they differ among themselves" (Majlisī, p. 244).

118 "From the powers of reason the proof of things is derived, and through these powers God makes known to the reason, or to its possessor, the acknowledgment of Him" (Majlisī, p. 244).

119 'Sincerity' is to make the knowledge of Him pure from all that is not appropriate to His sacred Essence, i.e., materiality, accidentality, extraneous attributes (*al-ṣifāt al-zā'idah*) and temporal phenomena. To say that he means 'sincerity in devotion' would be artificial and forced (*takalluf*)" (Majlisī, p. 244). In the Quran the chapter called "Sincerity" (*al-ikhlāṣ*) is also called "The Profession of Unity" (*al-tawḥīd*), and the meaning of sincerity in Islam is tied to the correct profession of divine Unity in terms of the negation of all "Associationism" (*shirk*). The meaning of sincerity is discussed most profoundly perhaps in Sufi writings, where it means complete negation of self. See F. Schuon, *Understanding Islam*, pp. 140, 155-6.

120 "I.e., whoso affirms that He possesses extraneous attributes does not negate an understanding of Him in terms of comparison" (Majlisī, p. 244).

121 That is, if these temporal events and changes referred to Him they would indicate that He had been created, and He would then be proof of another Creator, just as possible beings are proof of the Necessary Being (Majlisī, p. 246).

122 There is no substance to the absurd arguments that would prove Him temporal and possessed of extraneous attributes, and no answer to such arguments precisely because of their self-evident absurdity. By saying such things one does not glorify Him, rather one attributes to Him imperfection (Majlisī, p. 246).

123 According to Majlisī this means that there is nothing wrong with distinguishing Him from creation, unless we consider a perfection — His lying above duality and beginning — to be a fault. He cites the following line of poetry as an example of this type of expression: "They have no fault except that their swords/ Are dented from slashing the enemy forces". I.e., their only "fault" is a perfection (p. 246).

Another possible interpretation of this passage, which however is made doubtful by the context and structure of this and other sayings of the Imams, is to say that there is always something provisional about distinguishing God from creation, for this implies some sort of fundamental duality, which precisely — as asserted by the Shahādah, *lā ilāha illallāh* — God transcends. The world cannot exist "independently" of God, otherwise it would be another deity. If God is one, then ultimately the world cannot be other than He. Certainly He is other than the world, however, as this and all the other *ḥadīths* cited from the *Biḥār al-anwār* emphasize so strongly. See F. Schuon, *Understanding Islam*, pp. 17-18 and 125-6.

124 Cf. such Quranic passages as the following: "Whoso associates with God anything, has gone astray into far error . . . Whoso takes Satan to him for a

friend, instead of God, has surely suffered a manifest loss" (IV, 116-9).

125 The *zanādiqah* (sing.: *zindīq*) are identified specifically in Islamic history with the Manichaeans, but the word is also used more generally, as here, to mean unbeliever and heretic.

126 Concerning the use of the term "thing" to refer to God, see above, note 92.

127 Majlisī comments on the unbeliever's question and the Imam's answer as follows (p. 38): "The apparent meaning is that he is asking about the beginning of God's being and existence. But it is also possible that the question concerns the principle of time for His existence. According to the first (possibility), the gist of his answer is that beginning in time pertains to that which is temporal, to that which had been nonexistent and then became existent. But as for God, nonexistence is impossible (so He cannot have a beginning in time).

"According to the second (possibility), the meaning is that the existent in time would be so through transformation in essence and attributes, for time is the relationship of the changing (*al-mutaghayyir*) to the changing. So in one moment of time it has a state which it does not have in another. But God transcends change in essence and attributes."

128 Cf. Quran XIII, 12.

129 Cf. Quran II, 164.

130 I.e., He is not veiled, for He sees all things. It is men who have veiled themselves from Him.

131 These are all divine names which occur in the Quran. It should be noted, however, that the name *laṭīf* ("Subtle") is particularly difficult to render into English in a manner which would do justice to its various shades of meaning, as will be apparent from the passage. Nevertheless it seemed better to maintain the one word in English than to try to change it according to context and lose the point which the Imam wishes to make. In another *ḥadīth* Imam Riḍā explains the meaning of the divine name *al-laṭīf* as follows: God is "*Laṭīf*, not because of being scanty, slender or small, but because of penetrating into things and being impossible of comprehension .... God is too subtle to be grasped within a definition or limited by a description, whereas, 'subtlety' for us is in smallness of size and quantity" (*al-Tawḥīd*, p. 189).

132 "Wisdom" (*al-ḥikmah*) is defined as "knowledge which puts everything in its place", and therefore implies application and "workmanship".

133 Here subtle and majestic, *laṭīf* and *jalīl*, are meant to be two contrasting attributes, referring to the very small and the very large, etc.

134 Cf. Quran VI, 59: "With Him are the keys of the Unseen; none knows them but He. He knows what is in land and sea; not a leaf falls, but He knows it. Not a grain in the earth's shadows, not a thing, fresh or withered, but it is in a Book Manifest."

PART II

THE RULER AND SOCIETY

Professing God's Unity and accepting Muhammad as His prophet bring in their wake innumerable consequences. If the Quran is God's Word and Muhammad His chosen messenger who "speaks out not of caprice" (LIII, 3), their instructions concerning all things must be obeyed. Faced with these facts of their faith, the Muslims soon developed a complicated science of the *Sharīʿah* or Divine Law, a science which embraces every dimension of human conduct, including the political.

One of the earliest and best expositions of Islam's explicit and implicit instructions concerning government and its role in society is ʿAlī's instructions to Mālik ibn al-Ḥārith al-Nakhaʿī, surnamed al-Ashtar ("the man with inverted eyelashes") because of a wound he received in battle. He was one of the foremost Muslim warriors in the first few years of Islam's spread and one of ʿAlī's staunchest supporters. He advised ʿAlī against making a truce with Muʿāwiyah at the battle of Ṣiffīn and was poisoned on his way to assume his post as governor of Egypt in the year 37/658 or 38/659, shortly after ʿAlī became caliph following the assassination of ʿUthmān.[1]

Since these instructions form part of ʿAlī's *Nahj al-balāghah*, they have been discussed by all the more than 100 commentators on the text. I have made extensive use of two of the most famous of the commentaries. The first is by Ibn Abi-l-Ḥadīd (d. 655/1257), a historian who was attached to the Abbasid court in Baghdad. His commentary is one of the earliest, and because of its thoroughness and exactitude forms the basis for many of the later commentaries. The second is by Ibn Maytham al-Baḥrānī, a well-known

Shi'ite scholar and theologian who died in 679/1282-3. In addition I have profited from the glosses of the nineteenth century reformer Muḥammad ᶜAbduh (d. 1905) and one or two other modern commentaries which are mentioned in the notes.

ᶜAlī's Instructions to Mālik al-Ashtar

ᶜAlī wrote these instructions to al-Ashtar al-Nakhaᶜī when he appointed him governor of Egypt and its provinces at the time the rule of Muḥammad ibn Abī Bakr was in turmoil. It is the longest set of instructions (in the *Nahj al-balāghah*). Among all his letters it embraces the largest number of good qualities.

Part One: Introduction[2]

In the Name of God, the Merciful, the Compassionate

This is that with which ᶜAlī, the servant of God and Commander of the Faithful, charged Mālik ibn al-Ḥārith al-Ashtar in his instructions to him when he appointed him governor of Egypt: to collect its land tax,[3] to war against its enemies, to improve the condition of the people and to engender prosperity in its regions. He charged him to fear God, to prefer obedience to Him (over all else) and to follow what He has directed in His Book — both the acts He has made obligatory and those He recommends[4] — for none attains felicity but he who follows His directions, and none is overcome by wretchedness but he who denies them and lets them slip by. (He charged him) to help God — glory be to Him — with his heart, his hand and his tongue,[5] for He — majestic is His Name — has promised to help him who exalts Him.[6] And he charged him to break the passions of his soul and restrain it in its recalcitrance, for the soul incites to evil, except inasmuch as God has mercy.[7]

Part Two: Commands and Instructions Concerning Righteous Action in the Affairs of the State

Know, O Mālik, that I am sending you to a land where governments, just and unjust, have existed before you. People will look upon your affairs in the same way that you were wont to look upon the affairs of the rulers before you. They will speak about you as you were wont to speak about those rulers. And the righteous are only known by that which God causes to pass concerning them on the tongues of His servants. So let the dearest of your treasuries be the treasury of righteous action. Control your desire and restrain your soul from what is not lawful to you, for restraint of the soul is for it to be equitous in what it likes and dislikes. Infuse your heart with mercy, love and kindness for your subjects. Be not in face of them a voracious animal, counting them as easy prey, for they are of two kinds: either they are your brothers in religion or your equals in creation. Error catches them unaware, deficiencies overcome them, (evil deeds) are committed by them intentionally and by mistake. So grant them your pardon and your forgiveness to the same extent that you hope God will grant you His pardon and His forgiveness. For you are above them, and he who appointed you is above you, and God is above him who appointed you. God has sought from you the fulfillment of their requirements and He is trying you with them.

Set yourself not up to war against God,[8] for you have no power against His vengeance, nor are you able to dispense with His pardon and His mercy. Never be regretful of pardon or rejoice at punishment, and never hasten (to act) upon an impulse if you can find a better course. Never say, "I am invested with authority, I give orders and I am obeyed," for surely that is corruption in the heart, enfeeblement of the religion and an approach to changes (in fortune). If the authority you possess engender in you pride or arrogance, then reflect upon the tremendousness of the dominion of God above you and His power over you in that in which you yourself have no control. This will subdue your recalcitrance, restrain your violence and restore in you what has left you of the power of your reason. Beware of vying with God in His tremendousness and likening yourself to Him in His exclusive power, for God abases every tyrant and humiliates all who are proud.

See that justice is done towards God[9] and justice is done towards the people by yourself, your own family and those whom you favor among your subjects. For if you do not do so, you have worked wrong. And as for him who wrongs the servants of God, God is his adversary, not to speak of His servants. God renders null and void the argument of whosoever contends with Him. Such a one will be God's enemy until he desists or repents. Nothing is more conducive to the removal of God's blessing and the hastening of His vengeance than to continue in wrongdoing, for God harkens to the call of the oppressed and He is ever on the watch against the wrongdoers.[10]

Let the dearest of your affairs be those which are middlemost in rightfulness,[11] most inclusive in justice and most comprehensive in (establishing) the content of the subjects. For the discontent of the common people invalidates the content of favorites, and the discontent of favorites is pardoned at (the achievement of) the content of the masses. Moreover, none of the subjects is more burdensome upon the ruler in ease and less of a help to him in trial than his favorites. (None are) more disgusted by equity, more importunate in demands, less grateful upon bestowal, slower to pardon (the ruler upon his) withholding (favor) and more deficient in patience at the misfortunes of time than the favorites. Whereas the support of religion, the solidarity of Muslims and preparedness in the face of the enemy lie only with the common people of the community, so let your inclination and affection be toward them.

Let the farthest of your subjects from you and the most hateful to you be he who most seeks out the faults of men. For men possess faults, which the ruler more than anyone else should conceal. So do not uncover those of them which are hidden from you, for it is only encumbent upon you to remedy what appears before you. God will judge what is hidden from you. So veil imperfection to the extent you are able; God will veil that of yourself which you would like to have veiled from your subjects. Loose from men the knot of every resentment, sever from yourself the cause of every animosity, and ignore all that which does not become your station. Never hasten to believe the slanderer, for the slanderer is a deceiver, even if he seems to be a sincere advisor.

Bring not into your consultation a miser, who might turn you away from liberality and promise you poverty;[12] nor a coward, who might enfeeble you in your affairs; nor a greedy man, who might in his lust deck out oppression to you as something fair. Miserliness, cowardliness and greed are diverse temperaments which have in common distrust in God.[13]

Truly the worst of your viziers are those who were the viziers of the evil (rulers) before you and shared with them in their sins. Let them not be among your retinue, for they are aides of the sinners and brothers of the wrongdoers. You will find the best of substitutes for them from among those who possess the like of their ideas and effectiveness but are not encumbranced by the like of their sins and crimes; who have not aided a wrongdoer in his wrongs nor a sinner in his sins. These will be a lighter burden upon you, a better aid, more inclined toward you in sympathy and less intimate with people other than you. So choose these men as your special companions in privacy and at assemblies. Then let the most influential among them be he who speaks most to you with the bitterness of the truth and supports you least in activities which God dislikes in His friends, however this strikes your pleasure. Cling to men of piety and veracity. Then accustom them not to lavish praise upon you nor to (try to) gladden you by (attributing to you) a vanity you did not do,[14] for the lavishing of abundant praise causes arrogance and draws (one) close to pride.

Never let the good-doer and the evil-doer possess an equal station before you, for that would cause the good-doer to abstain from his good-doing and habituate the evil-doer to his evil-doing. Impose upon each of them what he has imposed upon himself.[15]

Know that there is nothing more conducive to the ruler's trusting his subjects than that he be kind towards them, lighten their burdens and abandon coercing them in that in which they possess not the ability. So in this respect you should attain a situation in which you can confidently trust your subjects, for trusting (them) will sever from you lasting strain.[16] And surely he who most deserves your trust is he who has done well when you have tested him, and he who most deserves your mistrust is he who has done badly when you have tested him.

Abolish no proper custom (*sunnah*) which has been acted upon by the leaders of this community, through which harmony has been strengthened and because of which the subjects have prospered. Create no new custom which might in any way prejudice the customs of the past, lest their reward belong to him who originated them, and the burden be upon you to the extent that you have abolished them.

Study much with men of knowledge (*ʿulamāʾ*) and converse much with sages (*ḥukamāʾ*) concerning the consolidation of that which causes the state of your land to prosper and the establishment of that by which the people before you remained strong.[17]

Part Three: Concerning the Classes of Men

Know that subjects are of various classes, none of which can be set aright without the others and none of which is independent from the others. Among them are (1.) the soldiers of God, (2.) secretaries for the common people and the people of distinction,[18] executors of justice[19] and administrators of equity and kindness,[20]

(3.) payers of *jizyah*[21] and land tax, namely the people of protective covenants[22] and the Muslims, (4.) merchants and craftsmen and (5.) the lowest class, the needy and wretched. For each of them God has designated a portion, and commensurate with each portion He has established obligatory acts (*farīḍah*) in His Book and the Sunnah of His Prophet — may God bless him and his household and give them peace — as a covenant from Him maintained by us.[23]

Now soldiers, by the leave of God, are the fortresses of the subjects, the adornment of rulers, the might of religion and the means to security. The subjects have no support but them, and the soldiers in their turn have no support but the land tax which God has extracted for them, (a tax) by which they are given the power to war against their enemy and upon which they depend for that which puts their situation in order and meets their needs. Then these two classes (soldiers and taxpayers) have no support but the third class, the judges, administrators and secretaries, for they draw up contracts,[24] gather yields, and are entrusted with private and public affairs. And all of these have no support but the merchants and craftsmen, through the goods which they bring together and the markets which they set up. They provide for the needs (of the first three classes) by acquiring with their own hands those (goods) to which the resources of others do not attain. Then there is the lowest class, the needy and wretched, those who have the right to aid and assistance. With God there is plenty for each (of the classes). Each has a claim upon the ruler to the extent that will set it aright. But the ruler will not truly accomplish what God has enjoined upon him in this respect except by resolutely striving, by recourse to God's help, by reconciling himself to what the truth requires and by being patient in the face of it in what is easy for him or burdensome.

(1.) Appoint as commander from among your troops that person who is in your sight the most sincere in the way of God and His Prophet and of your Imam,[25] who is purest of heart and most outstanding in intelligence, who is slow to anger, relieved to pardon, gentle to the weak and harsh with the strong and who is not stirred to action by severity nor held back by incapacity. Then hold fast to men of noble descent and those of righteous families and good precedents, then to men of bravery, courage, generosity and magnanimity, for they are encompassed by nobility and embraced by honor.

Then inspect the affairs of the soldiers[26] as parents inspect their own child. Never let anything through which you have strengthened them distress you, and disdain not a kindness you have undertaken for them, even if it be small, for it will invite them to counsel you sincerely and trust you. Do not leave aside the examination of their minor affairs while depending upon (the examination of) the great, for there is a place where they will profit from a trifling kindness, and an occasion in which they cannot do without the great.

Among the chiefs of your army favor most him who assists the soldiers with his aid and bestows upon them what is at his disposal to the extent that suffices both them and the members of their families left behind.[27] Then their concern in battle with the enemy will be a single concern, for your kind inclination toward them will incline their hearts to you.[28] Verily the foremost delight of the eye for rulers is the establishment of justice in the land and the appearance of love for them among the subjects.[29] But surely the subjects' love will not appear without the well-being of their breasts, and their sincerity (toward rulers) will not become free from blemishes unless they watch over their rulers, find their governments of little burden and cease to hope that their period (of rule) will soon come to an end. Therefore let their hopes be expanded, and persist in praising them warmly and takingin to account the (good) accomplishments of everyone among them who has accomplished, for frequent mention of their good deeds will encourage the bold and rouse the indolent, God willing.

Then recognize in every man that which he has accomplished, attribute not one man's accomplishment to another and fall not short (of attributing) to him the full extent of his accomplishment. Let not a man's eminence invite you to consider as great an accomplishment which was small, nor a man's lowliness to consider as small an accomplishment which was great.

Refer to God and His Messenger any concerns which distress you and any matters which are obscure for you, for God — high be He exalted — has said to a people whom He desired to guide, "O believers, obey God, and obey the Messenger and those in authority among you. If you should quarrel on anything, refer it to God and the Messenger" (IV, 59). To refer to God is to adhere to the clear text of His Book,[30] while to refer to the Prophet is to adhere to his uniting (*al-jāmiᶜah*) Sunnah, not the dividing (*al-mufarriq*).[31]

(2a.) Then choose to judge (*al-ḥukm*) among men him who in your sight is the most excellent of subjects, i.e., one who is not beleaguered by (complex) affairs, who is not rendered ill-tempered by the litigants,[32] who does not persist in error, who is not distressed by returning to the truth when he recognizes it, whose soul does not descend to any kind of greed, who is not satisfied with an inferior understanding (of a thing) short of the more thorough, who hesitates most in (acting in the face of) obscurities, who adheres most to arguments, who is the least to become annoyed at the petition of the litigants, who is the most patient (in waiting) for the facts to become clear and who is the firmest when the verdict has become manifest; a man who does not become conceited when praise is lavished upon him and who is not attracted by temptation. But such (men) are rare.

Thereupon investigate frequently his execution of the law (*qaḍā'*) and grant generously to him that which will eliminate his lacks and through which his need for men will decrease. Bestow upon him that station near to you to which none of your other favorites may aspire, that by it he may be secure from (character) assassination before you by men of importance.[33] (In sum) study that (i.e., the selection of judges) with thorough consideration, for this religion was prisoner in the hands of the wicked, who acted with it out of caprice and used it to seek (the pleasures of) the present world.[34]

(2b.) Then look into the affairs of your administrators. Employ them (only after) having tested (them) and appoint them not with favoritism or arbitrariness, for these two (attributes) embrace different kinds of oppression and treachery.[35] Among them look for people of experience and modesty[36] from righteous families foremost in Islam,[37] for they are nobler in moral qualities, more genuine in dignity and less concerned with ambitious designs, and they perceive more penetratingly the consequences of affairs. Then bestow provisions upon them liberally, for that will empower them to set themselves aright and to dispense with consuming what is under their authority; and it is an argument against them if they should disobey your command or sully your trust.

Then investigate their actions. Despatch truthful and loyal observers (to watch) over them, for your investigation of their affairs in secret will incite them to carry out their trust faithfully and to act kindly toward the subjects. Be heedful of aides. If one of them should extend his hand in a treacherous act, concerning which the intelligence received against him from your observers concurs, and if you are satisfied with that as a witness, subject him to corporeal punishment and seize him for what befell from his action. Then install him in a position of degradation, brand him with treachery and gird him with the shame of accusation.

(3.) Investigate the situation of the land tax in a manner that will rectify the state of those who pay it, for in the correctness of the land tax and the welfare of the taxpayers is the welfare of others. The welfare of others will not be achieved except through them, for the people, all of them, are dependent upon the land tax and those who pay it. Let your care for the prosperity of the earth be deeper than your care for the collecting of land tax, for it will not be gathered except in prosperity. Whoever exacts land tax without prosperity has desolated the land and destroyed the servants (of God). His affairs will remain in order but briefly.

So if your subjects complain of burden,[38] of blight, of the cutting off of irrigation water, of lack of rain, or of the transformation of the earth through its being inundated by a flood or ruined by drought, lighten (their burden) to the extent you wish their affairs to be rectified. And let not anything by which you have lightened their burden weigh heavily against you, for it is a store which they will return to you by bringing about prosperity in your land and embellishing your rule. You will gain their fairest praise and pride yourself at the spreading forth of justice among them. You will be able to depend upon the increase in their strength (resulting) from what you stored away with them when you gave them ease; and upon their trust, since you accustomed them to your justice toward them through your kindness to them. Then perhaps matters will arise which afterwards they will undertake gladly if in these you depend upon them, for prosperity will carry that with which you burden it. Truly the destruction of the earth only results from the destitution of its inhabitants, and its inhabitants become destitute only when rulers concern themselves with amassing (wealth), when they have misgivings about the endurance (of their own rule)[39] and when they profit little from warning examples.

(2c.) Then examine the state of your secretaries and put the best of them in charge of your affairs.[40] Assign those of your letters in which you insert your strategems and secrets to him among them most generously endowed with the aspects of righteous moral qualities, a person whom high estate does not make reckless, that because of it he might be so bold as to oppose you in the presence of an assembly. (He should be someone) whom negligence will not hinder from delivering to you the letters of your administrators, nor from issuing their answers properly for you in that which he takes for you and bestows in your stead; a person who will not weaken a contract which he binds for you, nor will he be incapable of dissolving what has been contracted to your loss; a man who is not ignorant of the extent of his own value in affairs, for he who is ignorant of his own value is even more ignorant of the value of others.

Let not your choosing of them be in accordance with your own discernment, confidence and good opinion, for men make themselves known to the discernment of rulers by dissimulating and serving them well, even though beyond this there may be nothing of sincere counsel and loyalty. Rather examine them in that with which they were entrusted by the righteous before you. Depend upon him who has left the fairest impression upon the common people and whose countenance is best known for trustworthiness. This will be proof of your sincerity toward God and toward him whose affair has been entrusted to you.

Appoint to the head of each of your concerns a chief from among these men, (a person) who is neither overpowered when these concerns are great nor disturbed when they are many. Whatever fault of your secretaries you overlook will come to be attached to you.

(4.) Then make merchants and craftsmen — those who are permanently fixed, those who move about with their wares and those who profit from (the labor of) their own body[41] — your own concern, and urge others to do so,[42] for they are the bases of benefits and the means of attaining conveniences. They bring (benefits and conveniences) from remote and inaccessible places in the land, sea, plains and mountains, and from places where men neither gather together nor dare to go. (The merchants and craftsmen) are a gentleness from which there is no fear of calamity and a pacifity from which there is no worry of disruption.[43] Examine their affairs in your presence and in every corner of your land.

But know, nevertheless, that in many of them is shameful miserliness, detestable avarice, hoarding of benefits and arbitrariness in sales. This is a source of loss to all and a stain upon rulers. So prohibit hoarding (*iḥtikār*), for the Messenger of God — may God bless him and his household and give them peace — prohibited it.[44] Let selling be an openhanded selling, with justly balanced scales and prices which do not prejudice either party, buyer or seller.[45] As for him who lets himself be tempted to hoard after you have forbidden him (to do so), make an example of him and punish him, but not excessively.

(5.) Then (fear) God, (fear) God regarding the lowest class, the wretched, needy, suffering and disabled who have no means at their disposal, for in this class there is he who begs and he who is needy (but does not beg). Be heedful for God's sake of those rights of theirs which He has entrusted to you. Set aside for them a share of your treasury (*bayt al-māl*) and in every town a share of the produce of the lands of Islam taken as booty (*ṣawāfī al-islām*),[46] for to the farthest away of them belongs the equivalent of what belongs to the nearest.[47] You are bound to observe the right of each of them, so be not distracted from them by arrogance, for you will not be excused if, to attend to the very important affair, you neglect the trifling, So avert not your solicitude from them and turn not your face away from them in contempt.

Investigate the affairs of those (of the lowest class) who are unable to gain access to you, those upon whom eyes disdain to gaze and whom men regard with scorn. Appoint to attend exclusively to them a person whom you trust from among the godfearing and humble, and let him submit to you their affairs. Then act toward them in a manner that will absolve you before God on the day that you meet Him.[48] For among the subjects these are more in need of equity than others. In the case of each of them prepare your excuse with God by accomplishing for him his rightfully due (*al-ḥaqq*). Take upon yourself the upkeep of the orphans and aged from among those who have no means at their disposal and do not exert themselves in begging. (All of) this is a heavy burden upon rulers. The truth (*al-ḥaqq*), all of it, is a heavy burden. But God may lighten it for people who seek the final end, who admonish their souls to be patient and trust in the truth of God's promise to them.

Part Four: Commands and Prohibitions in Mālik al-Ashtar's Best Interest

Set aside for those who have requests (*ḥājāt*) from you a portion (of your time) in which you yourself are free to (attend) to them. Hold an open audience for them and therein be humble before God who created you. Keep the soldiers and aides who are your bodyguards and police away from them so that their spokesman may address you without stammering (in fear), for I heard the Messenger of God — may God bless him and his household and give them peace — say not (only) on one occasion, "No community shall be sanctified within which the rightfully due of the weak may not be taken from the strong without stammering (by the weak)". Furthermore suffer them to be coarse and faltering of speech and become not annoyed and angry with them. For that God will outspread the wings of His mercy over you and make binding for you the reward of having obeyed Him. Bestow what you bestow in a pleasant manner and refrain (from granting requests when you must) gracefully and while asking pardon.

Then there are certain of your affairs which you must take in hand personally. Among them is giving an ear to your administrators when your secretaries have been unable to find the correct solution, and among them is attending to the requests of men when presented to you because the breasts of your aides have been straitened by them.[49]

Each day perform the work of that day, for to each belongs what is proper to it. Set aside for yourself in what is between you and God the most excellent of these hours and the fullest of these portions, even though all of them belong to God if in them your intention is correct and because of them the subjects remain secure. In making your religion sincerely God's perform especially His obligations (*farā'iḍ*),[50] which pertain only to Him. So give to God of your body in your night and your day, and complete in a perfect manner, neither defectively nor deficiently, what brings you near to God, no matter what may befall your body (as a result).[51]

When you stand to lead men in the canonical prayers, neither drive (them) away (by praying too lengthily) nor mar (the prayer by performing it too quickly or faultily), for among men there are some who are ill and others who are needy. I asked the Messenger of God — may God bless him and his household and give them peace — when he sent me to the Yemen, "How shall I lead them in prayer?" He said, "Lead them in prayer as the weakest of them prays, and be merciful to the believers."

Furthermore, prolong not your seclusion (*iḥtijāb*) from your subjects, for rulers' seclusion from subjects is a kind of constraint and (results in) a lack of knowledge of affairs. Seclusion from them cuts rulers off from the knowledge of that from which they have been secluded. Then the great appears to them as small and the small as great. The beautiful appears as ugly and the ugly as beautiful. And the truth becomes stained with falsehood. The ruler is only a man. He does not know the affairs which men hide from him. There are no marks upon the truth by which the various kinds of veracity might be distinguished from falsehood.

Again, you are one of only two men: either you give generously in the way of the truth — then why seclude yourself from carrying out a valid obligation or performing a noble deed? Or else you are afflicted by niggardliness — then how quickly will men refrain from petitioning you when they despair of your generosity! Moreover, most requests men present to you are those which impose no burden upon you, such as a complaint against a wrong or the seeking of equity in a transaction.

Then surely the ruler has favorites and intimates, among whom there is a certain arrogation, transgression and lack of equity in transactions. Remove the substance of these (qualities) by cutting off the means of obtaining these situations. Bestow no fiefs upon any of your entourage or relatives, nor let them covet from you the acquisition of a landed estate[52] which would bring loss to the people bordering upon it in (terms of) a water supply or a common undertaking, the burden of which would be imposed upon them.[53] Its benefit would be for those (who acquired the fiefs) and not for you, and its fault would be upon you in this world and the next.

Impose the right (*al-ḥaqq*) upon whomsoever it is encumbent, whether he be related to you or not.[54] Be patient in this and look to your (ultimate) account (*muḥtasib*),[55] however this may effect your relatives and favorites. Desire the ultimate end in that of it (imposing the right) which weighs heavily against you, for its outcome will be praiseworthy.

If any of your subjects should suspect you of an injustice, explain to them your justification. By your explanation turn their suspicions away from yourself. Thereby you train your soul (*nafṣ*), act kindly to your subjects and justify (yourself) in a manner to attain your need, i.e., setting them in the way of the truth.

Never reject a peace to which your enemy calls you and in which is God's pleasure, for in peace there is ease for your soldiers, relaxation from your cares and security for your land. But be cautious, very cautious, with your enemy after (having made) peace with him, for the enemy may have drawn near in order to take advantage of (your) negligence. Therefore be prudent and have doubts about trusting your enemy in this (matter).

If you bind an agreement between yourself and your enemy or cloth him in a protective covenant (*dhimmah*), guard your agreement in good faith and tend to your covenant with fidelity. Make of yourself a shield before what you have granted,[56] for men do not unite more firmly in any of the obligations (imposed upon them) by God than in attaching importance to fidelity in agreements,[57] despite the division among their sects and the diversity of their opinions. The idolators (*al-mushrikūn*) had already adhered to that (honoring agreements) among themselves before the Muslims, by reason of the evil consequences of treachery that they had seen. So never betray your protective covenant, never break your agreement and never deceive your enemy, for none is audacious before God but a wretched fool. God has made His agreement and His protective covenant a security which He has spread among the servants by His mercy, and a sanctuary in whose impregnability they may rest and in whose proximity they may spread forth.[58] Within it there is no corruption, treachery or deceit.

Make not an agreement in which you allow deficiencies and rely not upon ambiguity of language[59] after confirmation and finalization (of the agreement). Let not the straitness of an affair in which an agreement before God is binding upon you invite you to seek its abrogation unjustly. For your patience in the straitness of an affair, hoping for its solution and the blessing of its outcome, is better than an act of treachery. You would fear the act's consequence and (you would fear) that a liability before God will encompass you, a liability from which you will not be exempted in this world or the next.

Beware of blood and spilling it unlawfully, for nothing is more deserving of vengeance (from God), greater in its consequence or more likely to (bring about) a cessation of blessing and the cutting off of (one's appointed) term than shedding blood unjustly. God — glory be to Him — on the Day of Resurrection will begin judgment among His servants over the blood they have spilt.[60] So never strengthen your rule by shedding unlawful blood, for that is among the factors which weaken and enfeeble it, nay, which overthrow and transfer it. You have no excuse before God and before me for intentional killing, for in that there is bodily retaliation.[61] If you are stricken by error, and your whip, your sword or your hand should exceed their bounds in punishment — for in striking with the fists and all that exceeds it there is killing — never let the arrogance of your authority prevent you from paying the relatives of the killed their rightfully due (*al-ḥaqq*).[62]

Beware of being pleased with yourself,[63] of reliance upon that of yourself which pleases you and of the love of lavish praise, for these are among Satan's surest opportunities to efface what there might be of the good-doers' good-doing.

Beware of reproaching (*mann*) your subjects in your good-doing (for their insufficient acknowledgment of their debt to you), of overstating the deeds you have done and of making promises to them followed by non-observance. For reproach voids good-doing,[64] overstatement takes away the light of the truth and non-observance results in the hatred of God and men. God — may He be exalted — has said, "Very hateful is it to God, that you say what you do not" (LXI, 3).

Beware of hurrying to (accomplish) affairs before their (proper) time, of neglecting them when they are possible, of stubborn persistence in them when they are impracticable and of weakness in them when they have become clear. So put everything in its place and perform every action at its time.

Beware of arrogating for yourself that in which men are equal; and of negligence in that which is of concern after it has become manifest to the eyes (of men), for these things will be held against you for (the benefit of) others;[65] and (beware of negligence) of the fact that little remains until the coverings of affairs are lifted from you and justice is demanded from you for the wronged.[66]

Control the ardor of your pride, the violence of your strength, the force of your hand and the edge of your tongue. Be on thy guard against all these by restraining impulses and delaying force until your anger has subsided and you have mastered (your own) power of choice. But you will not gain control over that from your soul until you multiply your concern for remembering the return unto your Lord.

Encumbent upon you is to recall the just governments, the excellent customs, the Sunnah of our Prophet—may God bless him and his household and give them peace—and the obligations (promulgated) in the Book of God, which preceded you among those of earlier times. Take as the model for your action what you have observed us to perform of them, and strive to your utmost to follow what I have instructed you in these my instructions. I trust in them to act as my argument against you so that you shall have no cause for your soul's hastening to its caprice.[67]

I ask God by the amplitude of His mercy, and His tremendous power to grant every desire, to bestow upon me and you in that wherein is His pleasure success in presenting Him and His creatures with a clear justification (for our actions). (May He bestow) excellent praise from among His servants, fair influence in the land, completion of blessings and manifold increase in honor. And (I ask) that He seal (the lives of) me and you with felicity (*al-saʿādah*) and martyrdom (*al-shahādah*). "Unto Him we are returning" (II, 156). Peace be upon the Messenger of God — may God bless him and his good and pure household and grant them abundant peace. *Wa-l-salām.*

NOTES

1 See the article "al-Ashtar" in the new *Encyclopedia of Islam*.

2 The division into parts and the headings of parts two, three and four are taken from the commentary of Ibn Maytham.

3 The land tax (*kharāj*) was collected on the basis of the land's produce. See the *Encyclopedia of Islam* (new edition), vol. 3, pp. 1030-56.

4 *Farā'iḍ wa sunan.* The first very often refer to those acts which are commanded by God — such as the five daily prayers, fasting during the month of Ramadan, etc. — in which case they are contrasted with the *sunan*, meaning the commands of the Prophet, which are divided into the commands he gave orally (*qawl*), the acts he performed (*fiᶜl*) and the acts he allowed others to perform without criticising or protesting (*iqrār*). Here, however, since both kinds of acts are said to be mentioned in the Quran, the meaning is as translated.

5 " 'With his heart', or through firm belief; 'with his hand', or through holy war and exertion in His path; and 'with his tongue', or through speaking the truth, commanding the good and forbidding the evil" (Ibn Abi-l-Ḥadīd, vol. 17, p. 31).

6 Cf. Quran XLVII, 7, "O believers, if you help God, He will help you and confirm your feet", and other similar verses, such as XXII, 40.

7 Nearly a direct quotation from Quran XII, 53: "Surely the soul incites to evil, except inasmuch as my Lord has mercy."

8 "I.e., oppose Him not through acts of disobedience" (Ibn Abi-l-Ḥadīd, vol. 17, p. 33).

9 "I.e., Perform for Him the worship which He has made encumbent upon you and the requirements of intelligence and tradition" (Ibn Abi-l-Ḥadīd, vol. 17, p. 35).

10 Cf. Quran LXXXIX, 14: "Surely the Lord is ever on the watch."

11 *Awsaṭuhā fi-l-ḥaqq*, reference to the "golden mean". Here some of the commentators mention Aristotle and refer to such *ḥadīths* of the Prophet as "The best of affairs is their middlemost." See for example T. al-Fakiki, *al-Rāᶜi wa-l-raᶜiyyah*, vol. 2, Najaf, 1940, pp. 108-11.

12 According to Ibn Abi-l-Ḥadīd, this sentence is based upon the following Quranic verse: "The devil promises you poverty and bids you unto indecency; but God promises you His pardon and His bounty" (II, 268). He explains that the commentators of the Quran say that here "indecency" (*al-faḥshā'*) means "miserliness" (*al-bukhl*), and that the meaning of "promises you poverty" is that he makes you believe you will become poor if you are generous with your

wealth (vol. 17, p. 41).

13 Ibn Abi-l-Ḥadīd comments that if man trusts God with certainty and sincerity, he will know that his life-span, his daily provision, his wealth and his poverty are foreordained and that nothing occurs but by God's decree (vol. 17, p. 41). Ibn Maytham points out that "distrust in God begins with lack of knowledge (*maᶜrifah*) of Him." A person ignorant of His generosity and bounty will not know that He rewards what is expended in His path; hence he will be miserly in order to avoid poverty. He makes similar remarks concerning the qualities of cowardliness and greed.

14 According to Ibn Maytham this sentence is part of the description of those favorites who should be most influential. It means that the ruler "should train and discipline them by forbidding them from praising him lavishly or trying to make him happy by a false statement in which they attribute to him an act which he did not do and by this attribution cause him to be blameworthy." He then quotes the following verse of the Quran: "Reckon not that those who rejoice in what they have brought, and love to be praised for what they have not done — do not reckon them secure from chastisement" (III, 188).

15 "The evil-doer has imposed upon himself worthiness for punishment and the good-doer worthiness for reward" (Muḥammad ᶜAbduh, vol. 3, p. 98).

16 Ibn Abi-l-Ḥadīd comments on this passage as follows: "Whoever does good toward you will trust you and whoever does evil will shy away from you. This is because when you do good to someone and repeat it, you will come to believe that he likes you, and this belief will in turn lead to your liking him, for man by his very nature likes anyone who likes him. Then when you like him, you will feel secure with him and trust him. The reverse is true when you do evil toward someone . . ." (vol. 17, p. 47).

17 "He commands him to multiply his study with the men of knowledge, i.e., he should increase his study of the injunctions of the *Shariᶜah* and the laws of religion; and he should increase his discussions with sages, or those whose knowledge is from God Himself (*al-ᶜārifūn billāh*) and who know the secrets of His servants and His land" (Ibn Maytham).

18 The secretaries (*kuttāb*) are "those who are in charge of the ruler's own affairs and who write letters for him to his administrators and commanders. They take care of making arrangements and running the government administration (*dīwān*)" (Ibn Abi-l-Ḥadīd, vol. 17, p. 76).

19 *Quḍāt al-ᶜadl*, i.e. judges.

20 Administrators (*ᶜummāl*) are government officials concerned with the affairs of "the general public, alms, religious endowments, the common interest, etc." (Ibn Abi-l-Ḥadīd, vol. 17, p. 69). For the meaning of the term *ᶜāmil* (singular of *ᶜummāl*) throughout Islamic history see the *Encyclopedia of Islam* (new edition), vol. 1, p. 435.

21 *Jizyah* is the head tax upon "People of the Book" — followers of revealed religions other than Islam — who live under Muslim rule.

22 *Ahl al-dhimmah*. In other words the "People of the Book" who live in Muslim lands and are accorded hospitality and protection by Islam on condition of acknowledging Islamic political domination and paying the *jizyah*.

23 The covenant between man and God (*ᶜahd*) is frequently mentioned in the Quran and plays a central role in Islamic thought. Some representative

Quranic verses are the following: "Only men possessed of minds remember, who fulfill God's covenant..." (XIII, 20); "And fulfill the covenant; surely the covenant shall be questioned of" (XVII, 34); "Made I not a covenant with you Children of Adam, that you should not serve Satan . . . and that you should serve Me?" (XXXVI, 59-60).

24 One commentator remarks as follows: "Land tax is only paid in accordance with an agreement between the owners of the land and the ruler, so it is necessary that the documents be drawn up. Furthermore officials have to collect the land tax from the land owners according to the terms of the contract. Here it is possible that disputes arise between the government officials and the landowners, so it will be necessary to refer to judges to solve these disputes." Mīrzā Ḥabīballāh al-Hāshimī, *Minjāj al-barāᶜah fī sharḥ nahj al-balāghah*, Tehran, 1389/1969-70, vol. 20, p. 200.

25 I.e., Imam ᶜAlī himself.

26 "Of the soldiers" is a translation of the pronoun "their", and some question remains as to whether the pronoun does not in fact refer to the commanders. "If you say, 'But the soldiers of the army are not mentioned in the preceding section, only the commanders,' I will answer, 'On the contrary, they were mentioned where he says "The weak and the strong" ' " (Ibn Abi-l-Ḥadīd, vol. 17, p. 53.

27 *Khulūf* (plural of *khalf*) are the women, children and weak left behind when the men go on a journey.

28 Kind inclination toward the army means choosing for them the best of commanders, which will in turn cause them to love the ruler (Ibn Maytham).

29 According to Ibn-l-Ḥadīd, the context indicates that the word "subjects" refers in particular to the army. Al-Hāshimī disagrees and states that ᶜAlī does in fact mean all the subjects. He mentions them in the section on soldiers because the soldiers have to keep order in the land among the subjects (vol. 20, p. 222-2).

30 See above, p. 56, note 48.

31 The commentators explain this as meaning that people should follow that part of the Sunnah of the Prophet upon which all are agreed, not that concerning which there is a difference of opinion.

32 *Tamḥakuhu-l-khuṣūm*. According to Ibn Abi-l-Ḥadīd the verb here means to "make cantankerous or obstinate" (vol. 17, p. 59). Ibn Maytham, however, interprets the passage to mean that the judge should be someone "who is not overcome in his attempt to ascertain the truth by the obstinacy of the litigants. It has been said that this is an allusion to the person with whom the litigants are satisfied."

33 Muḥammad ᶜAbduh explains that when the judge is given an elevated position, the ruler's favorites as well as the common people will be in awe of him and no one will dare slander him, out of fear of the ruler and respect for the person held in such high esteem by him (vol. 3, p. 105).

34 Ibn Abi-l-Ḥadīd: "His words refer to the judges and rulers appointed by ᶜUthmān, for during his reign they did not judge rightfully but in accordance with caprice and in order to seek this world. Some people say that this happened because ᶜUthmān — may God's mercy be upon him — was weak and his relatives were able to gain mastery over him. They disrupted the affairs of state

without his knowledge, so the sin is upon them and ᶜUthmān is guiltless of what they were doing" (vol. 17, p. 60). See *Shiᶜite Islam*, pp. 46-48.

35 Ibn Abi-l-Ḥadīd reads *hum* for *humā*, i.e.: "For they (the administrators) are embraced by different kinds of oppression and treachery", and he interprets the sentence to refer to the administrators who served under the three caliphs before ᶜAlī. Al-Hāshimī offers a number of arguments in support of this interpretation, *Minhāj al-barāᶜah*, vol. 20, pp. 246-9.

36 "Experience (*tajribah*) alone is not sufficient if the administrator is not endowed with modesty (*ḥayā'*), for modesty is the basis of manliness (*murū'ah*). As the Prophet said, 'Modesty brings only good', and 'Whoso has not modesty has not religion and will not enter Paradise' . . ." (al-Fakīkī, *al-Rāᶜī wa-l-raᶜiyyah*, vol. 2, p. 38).

37 I.e., those families who were first to enter Islam. "This is because . . . . righteousness of family determines the way men are raised, and being foremost in Islam indicates nobility of character . . ." (*Ibid.*, p. 39).

38 Whether as the result of the land tax itself or the oppression of the tax-collectors (Ibn Abi-l-Ḥadīd, vol. 17, p. 72).

39 Ibn Abi-l-Ḥadīd offers two possible explanations of this clause. According to the first the words "*sū' ẓannihim bi-l-baqā'* " would have to be translated "they think wrongly about endurance", which means that they think their own existence will endure and they forget death and dissolution. In the translation, however, I have followed the second interpretation, which he explains as meaning "They imagine they will be deposed and replaced, so they seize upon opportunities, appropriate wealth and show no concern for the prosperity of the land" (vol. 17, p. 73).

40 "Know that the secretary alluded to by the Commander of the Faithful is he who nowadays is commonly called the 'vizier', for he is entrusted with the management of the affairs of the ruler's person and in all of them is his deputy. The letters of the administrators come to him and their answers are issued by him. He puts the (affairs of the) administrators in order and is supervisor over them. In fact he is the 'secretary of the secretaries' and for this reason is known as *the* vizier in the absolute sense. It is said that the secretary has three prerogatives before the king: to remove the veil from him (i.e., he has access to his personal affairs, even in the harem), to accuse traitors before him and to make secrets known to him . . ." (Ibn Abi-l-Ḥadīd, vol. 17, p. 79).

41 Ibn Abi-l-Ḥadīd explains that the first two of these groups are merchants — those who have shops and those who travel with their wares — and the third group are the craftsmen (vol. 17, p. 84).

42 The translation of this sentence is rather free and follows Ibn Abi-l-Ḥadīd's first interpretation. He adds that it is also permissible to read the sentence as follows: "Accept counsel (from me) for the good of merchants and craftsmen and counsel (others) concerning them" (vol. 17, pp. 83-4).

43 This is a literal translation of a passage which Ibn Abi-l-Ḥadīd explains as follows: "Then the Imam says, 'Surely they are a gentleness', that is to say, merchants and craftsmen are so. He seeks Mālik al-Ashtar's sympathy and favor for them and he says they are not like tax-collectors and commanders of the army, for they have to be sustained, protected and taken care of, the more so since there is no fear of calamity from them, neither in property where they

might be disloyal (as in the case of the tax-collectors) nor in the government where they might work corruption (as in the case of the commanders of the army)" (vol. 17, p. 84).

44 "According to the Sixth Imam, Jaᶜfar al-Ṣādiq (founder of the Jaᶜfarī, i.e. Twelve-Imam Shiʿite, school of law), 'It is reprehensible (*makrūh*) to hoard and to leave men with nothing. And it is said that it is forbidden (*ḥarām*), and this latter view is more correct. As was said by the Prophet of God, "Mercy is upon him who imports, and curses upon him who hoards". Surely hoarding is forbidden under two conditions: First, that food — i.e. wheat, barley, dates, raisins, clarified butter, or salt — be held back seeking an increase in price. Second, if there is no other distributor to be found . . .'." Quoted in al-Fakīkī, *al-Rāᶜī wa-l-raᶜiyyah*, vol. 2, p. 165.

45 Cf. Quran LXXXIII, 1-2: "Woe to the stinters who, when they measure against the people, take full measure, but, when they measure for them or weigh for them, they skimp."

46 Reference to the principle alluded to in the following verse of the Quran (VIII, 41): "Know that, whatever booty you take, the fifth of it is God's and the Messenger's and the near kinsman's and the orphan's and for the needy and the traveller".

47 "In other words, all poor Muslims are equal in their shares, there is no 'farthest away' or 'nearest'. Prefer not him who is near to you or to one of your favorites over him who is far from you and without any connection to you or reason for you to turn toward him. It is also possible that he means that the produce of the land taken as booty in a certain area should not be distributed only to the needy of that area, for the right to the produce of the land is the same whether a person is far from that land or resides in it" (Ibn Abi-l-Ḥadīd, vol. 17, pp. 86-7).

48 The "meeting with God" is mentioned in a number of Quranic verses, such as the following: "They indeed are losers who deny their meeting with God" (VI, 31).

49 " 'The breasts of aides are straitened' by expediting the removal of grievances. They love to postpone attending to them, either in order to seek personal gain or to demonstrate their own authority" (Muḥammad ᶜAbduh, vol. 3, p. 114).

50 i.e. the obligatory acts such as the five daily prayers.

51 The references to the body are due especially to the particularly physical nature of the daily canonical prayers. Ibn Abi-l-Ḥadīd explains the last clause as meaning, "Even if that wearies you and impairs your body and your strength" (vol. 17, p. 90).

52 The words "acquisition of a landed estate" (*iᶜtiqād ᶜuqdah*) might be translated literally as the "binding of a contract". The commentators, such as Ibn Abi-l-Ḥadīd (vol. 17, p. 97), Ibn Maytham and Muhammad ᶜAbduh (vol. 3, p. 11), explain it as translated (*iqtinā' ḍayᶜah* or *tamlīk ḍayᶜah*).

53 "His words . . . explain the methods of cutting off the causes referred to: the bestowal of a fief upon one of the entourage or a relative, and his desire to acquire a landed estate which will harm those people bordering upon it in terms of the water supply or a common undertaking — such as a building, etc. — while he imposes the burden of the undertaking on men, are the causes of the above-

mentioned situations . . ." (Ibn Maytham).

54 Or "whether near (*qarib*) to you or far away (*ba'id*)." I.e., whoever he might be, bring the person who has committed a wrong to justice.

55 I.e., realize that you will be rewarded in the next world.

56 "That is, even if you yourself should perish, act without treachery" (Ibn Abi-l-Ḥadīd, vol. 17, p. 107).

57 The importance of observing covenants and agreements is referred to frequently in the Quran. See for example, XVI, 91: "Fulfill God's covenant, when you make covenant, and break not the oaths after they have been confirmed . . .". See also VI, 153; XIII, 20; XVII, 34 et al.

58 According to Ibn Abi-l-Ḥadīd (vol. 17, p. 109), "in whose proximity they may spread forth" means "while dwelling in its proximity they may disperse in search of their needs and desires". ʿAbduh explains the verb translated here as "spread forth" (*yastafiḍūn*) to mean "swiftly take refuge" (vol. 3, p. 118), but the first interpretation seems more likely.

59 *Laḥn qawl*, "color of words". Ibn Maytham explains this expression as meaning "ambiguity, dissimulation or allusion." Ibn Abi-l-Ḥadīd's explanation is similar: "He forbids him when making an agreement between himself and his enemy to break it by relying upon a hidden interpretation or the tenor of the words, or by saying, 'Surely I meant such and such, I did not have the apparent sense of the words in mind' " (vol. 17, p. 109).

60 Ibn Abi-l-Ḥadīd cites the following *ḥadīth* of the Prophet: "On the Day of Resurrection the first thing which God will judge upon among the servants is blood which has been spilled" (vol. 17, p. 111).

61 "Then he advises him that intentional killing involves retaliation, and he says 'bodily retaliation'. In other words, intentional killing makes the destruction of the physical body necessary, just as you have destroyed the body of the person killed. The Imam's intention is to frighten him with these words, and they are more effective than if he had merely said, 'surely in that there is retaliation' " (Ibn Abi-l-Ḥadīd, vol. 17, p. 111).

62 Like retaliation in cases of intentional murder, compensation in cases of unintentional killing are determined by the *Sharīʿah*. Cf. Quran IV, 92-3: "It belongs not to a believer to slay a believer, except it be by error. If any slays a believer by error, then let him free a believing slave, and bloodwit is to be paid to his family unless they forego it as a freewill offering. If he belong to a people at enmity with you and is a believer, let the slayer set free a believing slave. If he belong to a people joined with you by a compact, then bloodwit is to be paid to his family and the slayer shall set free a believing slave . . . And whoso slays a believer wilfully, his recompense is Gehenna . . .".

63 Ibn Abi-l-Ḥadīd cites several sayings of the Prophet, including the following: "There are three mortal perils: yielding to niggardliness, following caprice and being pleased with oneself" (vol. 17, p. 114).

64 Cf. Quran II, 264: "O believers, void not your freewill offerings with reproach and injury."

65 Ibn Abi-l-Ḥadīd comments: For example, if it is pointed out to the commander that one of his favorites is performing a reprehensible act in secret, and if he then ignores that act, this will be to the benefit of the person doing the act, but not to his own benefit (vol. 17, p. 116).

66 Cf. Quran L, 19-22: "And death's agony comes in truth; that is what thou wast shunning! . . . 'Thou wast heedless of this; therefore We have now removed from thee thy covering, and so thy sight today is piercing'." Ibn Maytham remarks that when the veils of affairs are lifted from man at death, he sees the reality of these affairs and what God has prepared for him of good and evil: "The day every soul shall find what it has done of good brought forward, and what it has done of evil . . ." (Quran III, 30).

67 Cf. Quran LXXIX, 40-1: "But as for him who feared the Station of his Lord and forbade the soul its caprice, surely Paradise shall be the refuge."

PART III

THE SPIRITUAL LIFE: PRAYER AND SUPPLICATION

For the Muslim, the necessary personal concomitant of professing God's Unity is devotion to Him. The outward dimension of this devotion is shaped by the Shari'ite injunctions concerning worship: the canonical prayer, whether mandatory or recommended, fasting, pilgrimage, almsgiving, etc. But the inward dimension of Muslim devotions is much more difficult to grasp. Unlike the outward dimension, it cannot be defined in so many sentences. It can only be perceived through studying the lives and spiritual radiance of holy men and saints. Some of the most intimate glimpses of the pious Muslim soul are to be found in supplications.[1]

Prayer in Islam can be divided into four basic forms: canonical prayer (*ṣalāt*), supplication (*duʿā'*), litany (*wird*) and invocation (*dhikr*). One can say that the first — especially in its mandatory form — corresponds to what is implied in Christianity by mass or holy communion. The second is equivalent to "personal prayer", or simply to what the Christian often understands by the term "prayer" as such. The mandatory canonical prayer must be performed at specific times every day and according to strictly defined rules, while the recommended form also follows the same strict pattern (standing, bowing, prostrating, sitting, etc.). But one may "supplicate" God at any time and in any circumstance, without any set pattern or formulae. Supplications are strictly voluntary and "free". As for litanies and invocations — i.e., the recitation of Quranic formulae or one or more of the Names of

God — like supplication these are voluntary, although they are not so "free" since they follow set patterns, and like the canonical prayer, must be in Arabic. Litanies may be performed by any pious Muslim, whereas invocations are recited almost exclusively by the Sufis.

Although supplications left by the great saints of early Islam are of the type of "free prayer", invariably they have one element in common: since they were recited in Arabic (although they may be made in any language), they are largely inspired by Quranic images and incorporate Quranic verses and formulae. Also, they are usually rhythmic and very often — as in all four prayers translated here — employ rhymed prose (*sajᶜ*). Hence in this part I have divided the lines of the translation in keeping with the rhythm of the original in order to give a better idea of the style.

The author of the first supplication is Imam Ḥusayn, the Third Imam, who was martyred at Karbala and is probably the most important Imam in popular Shi'ite devotion. Certainly the days of mourning for him (in particular *tāsūᶜā* and *ᶜāshūrā*, the ninth and tenth of Muḥarram), are still the most solemn and carefully observed holidays in the Shi'ite calendar. Imam Ḥusayn made his supplication — one of the most famous in Shi'ite annals — one year during the pilgrimage to Mecca on the Day of ᶜArafah (the ninth of Dhu-l-ḥijjah), and it has been recited by pious Shi'ites ever since. On that day pilgrims pass the time at Mount Arafat occupying themselves with canonical prayer, reciting the Quran, litanies, invocations and supplications. The spirit of the day is well represented in the Imam's prayer.

The second and third prayers are taken from the Fourth Imam's *al-Ṣaḥīfat al-sajjādiyyah*, referred to in the introduction (p.9).

As for the fourth and final prayer, it was given by the Twelfth Imam to his second "deputy" (*nā'ib*), Abū Jaᶜfar Muḥammad ibn ᶜUthmān ibn Saᶜīd, who acted as the Imam's spokesman for many years until his death in 304/916-7 or 305/917-8. Here it is important for those not familiar with Shi'ite doctrines to understand that after the Twelfth Imam went into "occultation" at a young age in the year 260/873-4 and thus disappeared from the eyes of men, he maintained contact with four persons in succession until the last of them died in the year 329/940-1. Then his "greater occultation" (*al-ghaybat al-kubrā*) began. He will not reveal himself again until the end of time.[2]

A. al-Ḥusayn, the Third Imam

Prayer for the Day of ᶜArafah

Praise belongs to God

whose decree none may avert,
and whose gift none may prevent.
No fashioner's fashioning is like His fashioning,
and He is the Generous, the All-embracing.
He brought forth the varieties of unprecedented creatures
and perfected through His wisdom all He had fashioned.
Hidden not from Him are harbingers,
nor lost with Him are deposits.[3]
He repays every fashioner,
feathers the nest of all who are content
and has mercy upon all who humble themselves.
He sends down benefits
and the all-encompassing Book
in radiant light.
He hears supplications,
averts afflictions,
raises up in degrees,
and knocks down tyrants.
For there is no god other than He,
nothing is equal to Him,
"Like Him there is naught,
and He is the Hearing, the Seeing" (XLII, 11),
the subtle, the Aware,
and "He is powerful over all things" (V, 120 etc.).
O God, I make Thee my quest
and bear witness to Thy Lordship,
acknowledging that Thou art my Lord
and to Thee is my return.[4]
Thou originated me by Thy blessing before I was a thing remembered.[5]
Thou created me from dust,
then gavest me a place in the loins (of my fathers),
secure from the uncertainty of Fate and the vagaries of

the ages and the years.
I remained a traveller from loin to womb in a time
immemorial of past days
and bygone centuries.
In Thy tenderness, bounty and goodness toward me Thou
didst not send me out into the empire of the
leaders of disbelief, those who broke Thy
covenant and cried lies to Thy messengers.[6]
Rather, Thou sentest me out to that guidance which had
been foreordained for me, the way which
Thou madest easy for me
and in which Thou nurtured me.
And before that Thou wert kind to me through Thy
gracious fashioning
and abundant blessings.
Thou originated my creation from a sperm-drop spilled[7]
and madest me to dwell in a threefold gloom among flesh,
blood and skin.[8]
Thou gavest me not to witness my creation,[9]
nor didst Thou entrust me with anything of my own affair.
Then thou sentest me out into the world for the guidance
that had been foredained for me, complete
and unimpaired.
Thou watched over me in the cradle
as an infant boy,
provided me with food,
wholesome milk,
and turned the hearts of the nurse-maids toward me.
Thou entrusted my upbringing to compassionate mothers,
guarded me from the calamities brought by the jinn
and kept me secure from excess and lack.
High art Thou, O Merciful! O Compassionate!
Then when I began to utter speech
Thou completed for me Thy abundant blessings.
Thou nurtured me more and more each year
until, when my nature was perfected
and my strength balanced,
Thou madest Thy argument encumbent upon me by
inspiring me with knowledge of Thee,
awing me with the marvels of Thy wisdom,

awakening me to the wonders of Thy creation which Thou
hadst multiplied in Thy Heaven and Thy earth,[10]
and instructing me in Thy thanks and remembrance.
Thou madest encumbent upon me Thy obedience and worship,
madest me to understand what Thy messengers had brought
and madest easy for me the acceptance of Thy good pleasure.
Thou wast gracious to me in all of this, through Thy succour and kindness.
Then, since Thou created me from the best soil,[11]
Thou wert not satisfied, my God, that I should have one blessing without another.
Thou provided me with varieties of sustenance
and kinds of garments
and Thy tremendous — most tremendous — graciousness to me
and Thy eternal goodness toward me.
And finally, when Thou hadst completed for me every blessing
and turned away from me all misfortunes,
Thou wert not prevented by my ignorance and audacity
from guiding me toward that which would bring me nigh to Thee
or from giving me success in that which would bring me close to Thee.
For if I prayed to Thee Thou answered,
if I asked of Thee Thou gavest,
if I obeyed Thee Thou showed Thy gratitude,
and if I thanked Thee Thou gavest me more.[12]
All of that was to perfect Thy blessings upon me and Thy goodness toward me.
So glory be to Thee; Glory be to Thee,
who are Producer and Reproducer,[13] Laudable, Glorious.
Holy are Thy Names and tremendous Thy bounties.
So which of Thy blessings, my God, can I enumerate by counting and mentioning?

For which of Thy gifts am I able to give thanks?
Since they, O Lord, are more than reckoners can count[14]
or those who entrust to memory can attain by knowledge.
But the affliction and hardship, O God, that Thou turned
and averted from me
is more than the health and happiness that came to me.
And I witness, my God, by the truth of my faith,
the knotted resolutions of my certainty,
my pure and unadulterated profession of Unity,
the hidden inwardness of my consciousness,
the places to which the streams of light of my eyes
are attached,
the lines on my forehead's surface,
the openings for my breath's channels,
the parts of my nose's soft point,
the paths of my ears' canals,
what my lips close upon and compress,
the movements of my tongue in speaking,
the joint at the back of my mouth and jaw,
the sockets of my molar teeth,
the place where I swallow my food and drink,
that which bears my brain,
the hollow passages of my neck's fibers,
that which is contained in my breast's cavity,
the carriers of my aorta,
the places where my heart's curtain[15] is attached,
the small pieces of flesh around my liver,
that which the ribs of my sides encompass,
the sockets of my joints,
the contraction of my members,
the tips of my fingers,
my flesh,
my blood,
my hair,
my skin,
my nerves,
my windpipe,[16]
my bones,
my brain,
my veins,

and all of my members,
what was knitted upon them in the days when I was a suckling baby,
what the earth has taken away from me,
my sleep,
my waking,
my being still,
and the movements of my bowing and prostrating,
that had I taken pains and had I striven
for the duration of the epochs and ages
— were my life to be extended through them —
to deliver thanks for one of Thy blessings,
I would not have been able to do so,
except by Thy grace, which alone makes encumbent upon me never-ending and ever renewed gratitude to Thee,
and fresh and ever present praise.
Indeed, and were I and the reckoners among Thy creatures ever so eager
to calculate the extent of Thy bestowal of blessings,
whether past
or approaching,
we would fail to encompass it through numbers
or to calculate its boundaries.
Never! How could it ever be done!
For Thou announcest in Thy eloquent Book
and truthful Tiding,
"And if you count God's blessing, you will never number it" (XIV, 34).
Thy Book, O God, Thy Message, has spoken the truth!
And Thy prophets and messengers delivered Thy revelation that Thou hadst sent down upon them
and the religion that Thou hadst promulgated for them and through them.
And I witness, my God, by my effort,
my diligence,
and the extent of my obedience and my capacity,
and I say as a believer possessing certainty,

"Praise belongs to God,
who has not taken to Him a son"
that He might have an heir,
"and who has not any associate in His dominion"
who might oppose Him in what He creates,
"nor any protector out of humbleness" (XVII, 111)
who would aid Him in what He fashions.
So glory be to Him,
glory be to Him!
"Why, were there gods in earth and heaven other than God,
they would surely go to ruin" (XXI, 22) and be rent.[17]
Glory be to God, the Unique, the One,
"the Everlasting Refuge" who "has not begotten, nor has He been begotten,
and equal to Him there is none" (CXII, 2-4).
Praise belongs to God,
praise equal to the praise of the angels stationed near to Him
and the prophets sent by Him.
And God bless His elect, Muhammad,
the Seal of the Prophets,
and his virtuous, pure and sincere household, and give them peace.

Then he began to supplicate. He occupied himself with prayer as tears ran from his blessed eyes. Then he said:

O God, cause me to fear Thee as if I were seeing Thee,[18]
give me felicity through piety toward Thee,
make me not wretched by disobedience toward Thee,
choose the best for me by Thy decree (*qaḍā'*)
and bless me by Thy determination (*qadar*),
that I may love not the hastening of what Thou hast delayed,
nor the delaying of what Thou hast hastened.
O God, appoint for me sufficiency in my soul,
certainty in my heart,
sincerity in my action,
light in my eyes,

and insight in my religion.
Give me enjoyment of my bodily members,
make my hearing and my seeing my two inheritors,
help me against him who wrongs me,
show me in him my revenge and my desires,
and console thereby my eyes.
O God, remove my affliction,
veil my defects,
forgive my offence,
drive away my Satan,[19]
dissolve my debt,
and give me, my God, the highest degree
in the world to come and in this world.
O God, to Thee belongs the praise,
just as Thou created me and made me to hear and to see;
and to Thee belongs the praise,
just as Thou created me and made me a creature unimpaired
as a mercy to me,
while Thou hadst no need of my creation.

My Lord, since Thou created me
and then made straight my nature;
my Lord, since Thou caused me to grow
and made good my shape;[20]
my Lord, since Thou didst good to me
and gavest me well-being in my soul;
my Lord, since Thou preserved me
and gavest me success;
my Lord, since Thou blessed me
and then guided me;
my Lord, since Thou chosest me
and gavest me of every good;
my Lord, since Thou gavest me to eat
and drink;[21]
my Lord, since Thou enriched me
and contented me;[22]
my Lord, since Thou aided me
and exalted me;

my Lord, since Thou clothed me with Thy pure covering
and smoothed the way for me by Thy sufficient fashioning:
Bless Muhammad and the household of Muhammad,
aid me against the misfortunes of time and the calamities of nights and days,
deliver me from the terrors of this world and the torments of the world to come
and spare me from the evil of that which the evildoers do in the earth.

O God, as for what I fear, spare me from it,
and as for what I seek to avoid, guard me against it.
In my soul and my religion watch over me,
in my travelling protect me,
in my family and my property appoint for me a successor,
in what Thou hast provided for me bless me,
in my soul humble me,
in the eyes of men magnify me,
from the evil of jinn and men preserve me,
for my sins disgrace me not,
for my inward secrets shame me not,
for my action try me not,
of Thy blessings deprive me not
and to other than Thee entrust me not.
My God, to whom wouldst Thou entrust me?
To a relative? He would cut me off.
Or to a stranger? He would look at me with displeasure.
Or to those who act toward me with arrogance?
But Thou art my Lord and the sovereign over my affair.
I would complain to Thee of my exile and the remoteness of my abode,
and that he whom Thou hast made sovereign over me despises me.
My God, so cause not Thy wrath to alight upon me.
If Thou becomest not wrathful with me
I will have no care[23] — glory be to Thee!
But Thy protection is more embracing.
So I ask Thee, O Lord, by the Light of Thy Face by which the

earth and the heavens are illuminated,
shadows are removed,
and the affairs of the ancients and the later folk are set aright,
not to cause me to die when Thy wrath is upon me,[24]
nor to send down upon me Thy anger.
The pleasure is Thine!
The pleasure is Thine,
to be satisfied with me before that.

There is no god but Thou, Lord of the Holy Land,[25]
the Sacred Monument,[26]
and the Ancient House,[27]
upon which Thou caused blessing to descend
and which Thou madest a sanctuary for mankind.[28]

O He who pardons the greatest sins by His clemency!
O He who lavishes blessings by His bounty!
O He who gives abundance by His generosity!
O Sustenance to me in my adversity!
O Companion to me in my solitude!
O Aid to me in my affliction!
O Benefactor to me in my blessing!
O my God
and God of my fathers,
Abraham, Ishmael, Isaac and Jacob![29]
Lord of Gabriel, Michael and Israfil![30]
Lord of Muhammad, the Seal of the Prophets,
and his household, the chosen ones!
Revealer of the Torah, the Gospel, the Psalms and the Criterion,[31]
and Sender down of *Kāf Hā' Yā' ᶜAyn Ṣād, Ṭā' Hā', Yā' Sīn*, and the Wise Quran![32]
Thou art my cave (of refuge) when the roads for all their amplitude constrict me
and the land for all its breadth is strait for me.
If not for Thy mercy, I would have been among the perishing,
and Thou annullest my slip.
If not for Thy covering me,[33] I would have been

among the disgraced,
and Thou confirmest me with help against my enemies.[34]
And if not for Thy helping me, I would have been
among those overcome.[35]

O He who appropriated loftiness and exaltation to Himself,
so His friends (*awliyā'*) are mighty through His might!
O He before whom kings place the yoke of abasement
around their necks,
for they fear His overwhelming power!
"He knows the treachery of the eyes and what the
breasts conceal" (XL, 19)
and the unseen brought by time and fate.
O He about whom none knows how He is but He!
O He about whom none knows what He is but He!
O He whom none knows but He!
O He who squeezed the earth onto the water and held
back the air with the sky!
O He to whom belong the noblest Names![36]
O He who possesses kindness which will never be cut off!
O He who assigned the cavalcade to Joseph in the barren
land,
brought him out of the well
and made him a king after slavery!
O He who returned him to Jacob after "his eyes were
whitened with sorrow that he was
suppressing" (XII, 84)![37]
O He who removed affliction and tribulation from Job[38]
and restrained Abraham's hands from the sacrifice of
his son after he had reached old age and
his life had passed by![39]
O He who answered the prayer of Zachariah
and bestowed upon him John,
not leaving him childless and alone![40]
O He who brought Jonah out from the stomach of the
fish![41]
O He who parted the sea for the Children of Israel,
then saved them
and drowned Pharoah and his hosts![42]
O He who sends winds heralding His mercy![43]

O He who does not hurry (to act) against those of His
creatures who disobey Him![44]
O He who rescued the sorcerers after (their) long denial!
They had early benefitted from His blessing,
eating His provision
and worshipping other than Him;
they had opposed, denied and cried lies to His
messengers.[45]
O God!
O God!
O Beginner, O Creator with no compeer!
O Everlasting who has no end!
O Living when nothing was alive!
O Quickener of the dead![46]
O "He Who is aware of the deserts of every soul"
(XIII, 33)!
O He toward whom my gratitude was little,
yet He deprived me not!
My transgression was great,
yet He disgraced me not!
He saw me committing acts of disobedience,
yet he made me not notorious!
O He who watched over me in childhood!
O He who provided for me in my adulthood!
O He whose favors toward me cannot be reckoned and
whose blessings cannot be repaid!
O He who has confronted me with the good and the fair,
and I have confronted Him with evil and disobedience
in return!
O He who led me to faith before I had come to know
gratitude for His gracious bestowal!
O He upon whom I called when I was sick
and He healed me,
when naked
and He clothed me,
when hungry
and He satisfied me,
when thirsty
and He gave me to drink,
when abased

and He exalted me,[47]
when ignorant
and He gave me knowledge,
when alone
and He increased my number,
when away
and He returned me,
when empty-handed
and He enriched me,
when in need of help
and He helped me,
and when rich
and He took not from me.
I refrained from (calling upon Thee in) all of that
and Thou caused me to begin (to call).
Thine are the praise and the gratitude!
O He who overlooked my slip,
relieved my distress,
heard my prayer,
covered my defects,
forgave my sins,
caused me to reach my desire,
and helped me against my enemy!
If I were to count Thy blessings, favors and generous acts of kindness
I would not be able to reckon them.[48]

O my Protector!
Thou art He who was gracious,
Thou art He who blessed,
Thou art He who worked good,
Thou art He who was kind,
Thou art He who was bounteous,
Thou art He who perfected,
Thou art He who provided,
Thou art He who gave success,
Thou art He who bestowed,
Thou art He who enriched,
Thou art He who contented,[49]
Thou art He who sheltered,[50]

Thou art He who sufficed,
Thou art He who guided,
Thou art He who preserved (from sin),
Thou art He who covered (my sins),
Thou art He who forgave,
Thou art He who overlooked,
Thou art He who established (in the earth),[51]
Thou art He who exalted,
Thou art He who aided,
Thou art He who supported,
Thou art He who confirmed,
Thou art He who helped,
Thou art He who healed,
Thou art He who gave well-being,
Thou art He who honored
— blessed art Thou
and high exalted!
So Thine is the praise everlastingly,
and Thine is gratitude enduringly and forever!
Then I, my God, confess my sins,
so forgive me for them.
I am he who did evil,
I am he who made mistakes,
I am he who purposed (to sin),
I am he who was ignorant,
I am he who was heedless,
I am he who was negligent,
I am he who relied (upon other than Thee),
I am he who premeditated,
I am he who promised,
I am he who went back on his word,
I am he who confessed (my sins)
and I am he who acknowledged Thy blessings upon me
and with me and then returned to my sins.
So forgive me for them,
O He who is not harmed by the sins of His servants
nor needs He their obedience.
He gives success through His aid and His mercy to
whomsoever of them works righteousness.
So praise belongs to Thee, My God and My Lord!

My God, Thou commanded me and I disobeyed
and Thou forbade me and I committed what Thou hadst forbidden.
I became such that I neither possessed any mark of guiltlessness
that I might ask forgiveness
nor any power
that I might be helped.
Then by what means shall I turn toward Thee, O my Protector!?
What, by my ears?
Or my eyes?
Or my tongue?
Or my hand?
Or my leg?
Are not all of them Thy blessings given to me?
And with all of them I disobey Thee, O my Protector!
Thine is the argument and the means against me.[52]

O He who veiled me (my sins) from fathers and mothers lest they drive me away,
from relatives and brothers lest they rebuke me,
and from kings lest they punish me!
If they had seen, O my Protector, what Thou hast seen from me,
they would not have given me respite,
they would have abandoned me
and cut me off.

So here I am, O my God,
before Thee O Lord,
humbled, abased, constrained, despised,
neither possessing guiltlessness that I might ask forgiveness
nor possessing power that I might be helped.
There is no argument with which I might argue,
nor can I say I committed not (sins) and worked not evil.
And denial, were I to deny — my Protector! — could hardly profit me.
How could it ever do that?
For all of my members are witness against me for what I have done.[53]

And I acted with certainty and without any doubt that
Thou wilt ask me about great affairs,
and that Thou art the equitable Judge who does no wrong.
Thy justice is deadly for me and I flee from Thy every just
act.
If thou chastisest me, O my God, it is for my sins after
Thy argument against me;
and if Thou pardonest me, it is by Thy clemency,
generosity and kindness.

"There is no god but Thou, glory be to Thee!
Truly I am one of the wrong-doers" (XXI, 87).
There is no god but Thou, glory be to Thee!
Truly I am one of those who pray forgiveness.
There is no god but Thou, glory be to Thee!
Truly I am one of those who profess Thy Unity.
There is no god but Thou, glory be to Thee!
Truly I am one of the fearful.
There is no god but Thou, glory be to Thee!
Truly I am one of those who are afraid.
There is no god but Thou, glory be to Thee!
Truly I am one of the hopeful.
There is no god but Thou, glory be to Thee!
Truly I am one of those who yearn.
There is no god but Thou, glory be to Thee!
Truly I am one of those who say "There is no god
but Thou".
There is no god but Thou, glory be to Thee!
Truly I am one of the petitioners.
There is no god but Thou, glory be to Thee!
Truly I am one of the glorifiers.
There is no god but Thou, glory be to Thee!
Truly I am one of those who magnify.
There is no god but Thou, glory be to Thee, my Lord,
and the Lord of my fathers, the ancients!

My God, this is my praise of Thee exalting Thy majesty,
my sincerity in remembering Thee by professing Thy
Unity,
and my acknowledgment of Thy bounties by
enumeration,

even though I acknowledge
that I cannot reckon them for their multitude,
their abundance,
their manifestness
and their existence from ancient times
until a present in which Thou hast never ceased to care for me through them
from when Thou created me and brought me into existence in the beginning of (my) life,
by enriching from poverty,
relieving affliction,
bringing ease,
removing hardship,
dispelling distress,
and (giving me) well-being in body
and soundness in religion.
Were all the world's inhabitants, both the ancients and the later folk, to assist me in attempting to mention Thy blessing,
I would not be able, nor would they, to do so.
Holy art Thou and high exalted,
a generous,
mighty,
merciful
Lord.
Thy bounties cannot be reckoned,
nor Thy praise accomplished,
nor Thy blessings repaid.
Bless Muhammad and the household of Muhammad,
complete Thy blessings upon us
and aid us in Thy obedience.
Glory be to Thee! There is no god but Thou.

O God, truly Thou hearest the destitute,
removest the evil,[54]
succourest the afflicted,
healest the sick,
enrichest the poor,
mendest the broken,
hast mercy upon the young

and helpest the old.
There is no Support other than Thee
and none powerful over Thee.
And Thou art the Sublime, the Great.
O Freer of the prisoner in irons!
O Provider of the infant child!
O Protection of the frightened refugee!
O He who has no associate and no assistant!
Bless Muhammad and the household of Muhammad,
and give me this evening the best of what Thou hast given
to and bestowed upon any of Thy servants,
whether a blessing Thou assignest,
a bounty Thou renewest,
a trial Thou avertest,
an affliction Thou removest,
a prayer Thou hearest,
a good deed Thou acceptest
or an evil deed Thou overlookest.
Truly Thou art gracious,
Aware of what Thou wilt,
and Powerful over all things!

O God, truly Thou art the nearest of those who are called,
the swiftest of those who answer,
the most generous of those who pardon,
the most openhanded of those who give
and the most hearing of those who are asked of.
O Merciful and Compassionate in this world and the next!
Like Thee none is asked of;
and other than Thee none is hoped for.
I prayed to Thee and Thou answered me,
I asked of Thee and Thou gavest to me,
I set Thee as my quest and Thou hadst mercy upon me,
I depended upon Thee and Thou delivered me,
I took refuge with Thee and Thou sufficed me,
O God, so bless Muhammad, Thy servant, messenger and
prophet,
and his good and pure household, all of them.
And complete Thy blessings upon us,
gladden us with Thy gift

and inscribe us as those who thank Thee and remember
Thy bounties.
Amen, amen, O Lord of all beings!
O God, O He who owned and then was all-powerful,
was all-powerful and then subjected,
was disobeyed and then veiled (the sin of disobedience),
and was prayed forgiveness and then forgave.
O Goal of yearning seekers
and utmost Wish of the hopeful!
O He who "encompasses everything in knowledge" (LXV, 12)
and embraces those who seek pardon in tenderness,
mercy and clemency!
O God, truly we turn towards Thee this evening,
which Thou honored and glorified through Muhammad,
Thy prophet and messenger,
the elect of Thy creation,
the faithful guardian of Thy revelation which bears good
tidings and warning and which is the light-
giving lamp[55]
which Thou gavest to those who surrender (*al-muslimīn*)
and appointed as a mercy to the world's inhabitants.[56]
O God, so bless Muhammad and the household of Muhammad,
just as Muhammad is worthy of that from Thee,
O Sublime!
So bless him and his elect, good and pure household, all
of them,
and encompass us in Thy pardon,
for to Thee cry voices
in diverse languages.
So appoint for us a share this evening, O God,
of every good which Thou dividest among Thy servants,
every light by which Thou guidest,[57]
every mercy which Thou spreadest,[58]
every blessing which Thou sendest down,
every well-being with which Thou clothest
and every provision which Thou outspreadest.[59]
O Most merciful of the merciful!
O God, transform us now into men successful,
triumphant,
pious,

and prosperous.
Set us not among those who despair,
empty us not of Thy mercy,
deprive us not of that bounty of Thine for which we hope,
and set us not among those deprived of Thy mercy,
nor those who despair of the bounty of Thy gift for which
we hope.
Reject us not with the disappointed,
nor those driven from Thy door.

O Most Magnanimous of the most magnanimous!
O Most Generous of the most generous!
Toward Thee we have turned having sure faith,
repairing to and bound for Thy Sacred House.[60]
So help is with our holy rites,
perfect for us our pilgrimage,
pardon us,
and give us well-being,
for we have extended toward Thee our hands
and they are branded with the abasement of confession.

O God, so give us this evening what we have asked of Thee
and suffice us in that in which we have prayed Thee to
suffice us,
for there is none to suffice us apart from Thee
and we have no lord other than Thee.
Put into effect concerning us is Thy decision,
encompassing us is Thy knowledge[61]
and just for us is Thy decree.
Decree for us the good
and place us among the people of the good!

O God make encumbent upon us through Thy magnanimity
the mightiest wage,
the most generous treasure
and the lastingness of ease.
Forgive us our sins, all of them,
destroy us not with those who perish,[62]
and turn not Thy tenderness and mercy away from us,
O Most Merciful of the merciful!

O God, place us in this hour among those
who ask of Thee and to whom Thou givest,

who thank Thee and whom Thou increasest,[63]
who turn to Thee in repentance and whom Thou acceptest[64]
and who renounce all of their sins before Thee and whom Thou forgivest,
O Lord of majesty and splendor!
O God, purify us,
show us the right way
and accept our entreaty.
O Best of those from whom is asked!
And O Most Merciful of those whose mercy is sought!

O He from whom is not hidden the eyelids' winking,
the eyes' glancing,
that which rests in the concealed,
and that which is enfolded in hearts' hidden secrets!
What, has not all of that been reckoned in Thy knowledge
and embraced by Thy clemency?
Glory be to Thee and high indeed art Thou exalted above what the evil-doers say!
The seven heavens and the earths and all that is therein praise Thee,
and there is not a thing but hymns Thy praise.[65]
So Thine is the praise, the glory and the exaltation of majesty,
O Lord of majesty and splendor,
of bounty and blessing
and of great favor!
And Thou art the Magnanimous, the Generous,
the Tender, the Compassionate.
O God, give me amply of Thy lawful provision,
bestow upon me well-being in my body and my religion,
make me safe from fear[66]
and deliver me from the Fire.
O God, devise not against me,[67]
lead me not on step by step,[68]
trick me not[69]
and avert from me the evil of the ungodly among jinn and men.

Then he lifted his head and eyes toward Heaven. Tears were flowing from his blessed eyes as if they were two waterskins, and he said in a loud voice:

O Most Hearing of those who hear!
O Most Seeing of those who behold!
O Swiftest of reckoners![70]
O Most Merciful of the merciful!
Bless Muhammad and the household of Muhammad,
the chiefs, the fortunate.
And, I ask of Thee, O God, my need.
If Thou grantest it to me,
what Thou holdest back from me will cause me no harm;
and if Thou holdest it back from me,
what Thou grantest me will not profit me.
I ask Thee to deliver me from the Fire.
There is no god but Thou alone,
Thou hast no associate.
Thine is the dominion,
and Thine is the praise,
and Thou art powerful over everything.
O my Lord!
O my Lord!

Then he said "O my Lord" over and over. Those who had been gathered around him, who had listened to all of his prayer and who had limited themselves to saying "amen" raised their voices in weeping. They stayed in his company until the sun went down, and then all of them loaded their mounts and set out in the direction of the Sacred Monument.[71]

B. ᶜAlī Zayn al-ᶜĀbidīn, the Fourth Imam

1. *In Praise of God*

Praise belongs to God, the First without a first before Him
and the Last without a last which might be after Him.
Beholders' eyes fall short of seeing Him

and depicters' imaginations fail to describe Him.
He originated the creatures by His power with an
origination
and fashioned them according to His desire with a
fashioning.
Then He made them walk the path of His will
and incited them[72] in the way of His love.
They have no power to keep back from that to which
He has put them forward,
nor can they go forward to that from which He has
kept them back.
He appointed to every soul (*rūḥ*) from among them a
known and determined sustenance from
His provision.
No diminisher can diminish (the portion of)
whomsoever He has increased,
and no increaser can increase whomsoever He has
diminished.
Then He set for every soul a fixed term in life
and appointed for him a determined end.
He walks towards it in the days of his life
and overtakes it through the years of his destiny
until, when he accomplishes his final act
and closes his life's account,
He seizes him for that towards which He had
called him,
either His abundant reward
or His terrible punishment,
"That He may reward those who do evil with that
which they have done,
and reward those who do good with goodness"
(LIII, 31),
as justice from Him.
Holy are His Names
and manifest His bounties!
"He shall not be questioned as to what He does,
but they will be questioned" (XXI, 23).

And praise belongs to God,
for, had He held back from His servants the knowledge

to praise Him for the repeated favors with which He tries them[73]
and the abundant blessings which He lavishes upon them,
they would have made free use of His favors without praising Him
and taken ease in His provision without thanking Him.
And had it been so,
they would have left the conditions of humanity for those of beastliness.
They would have been as He described in the clear text of His Book:[74]
"They are but as the cattle —
nay, but they are farther astray!" (XXV, 44).

And praise belongs to God for what He has made known to us of Himself,
for the gratitude towards Him which He has inspired in us,
for the doors of the knowledge of His lordship which He has opened for us,
for the sincerity towards Him in professing His Unity to which He has guided us,
and for the heresy and doubt concerning Him[75] which He has averted from us;
a praise whereby we may be given long life among those of His Creatures who praise Him
and outstrip those who outstrip toward His good-pleasure and pardon;
a praise whereby the darkness of the Interval[76] may be lit for us,
the Path of the Resurrection[77] smoothed for us
and our positions at the Stations of the Witnesses[78] made eminent —
on the day when "every soul will be compensated for what it has earned;
they shall not be wronged" (XLV, 22);
"the day a master shall avail nothing a client,
and they shall not be helped" (XLIV, 41);
a praise which will ascend from us to the most exalted of

the ᶜIlliyūn,[79]
in "a book inscribed,
witnessed by those brought nigh" (LXXXIII, 20-21);
a praise whereby our eyes may be at rest when vision is confounded[80]
and our faces whitened when skins are blackened;[81]
a praise whereby we may be delivered from God's painful Fire
unto God's noble proximity;
a praise whereby we may rival the angels stationed nigh unto Him
and join the prophets sent by Him
in the Abode of Everlasting Life which does not remove,
and in the place of His Honor which does not change.

And praise belongs to God, who chose for us the good qualities of creation
and granted us the good things of provision.[82]
He assigned to us excellence through domination over all creation.
Each of His creatures submits to us through His power
and becomes obedient to us through His might.[83]

And praise belongs to God, who locked to us the door of need except toward Himself.
So how can we voice His praise?
And when can we thank Him?
Nay, when?[84]

And praise belongs to God, who set in us the organs of expansion,
appointed for us the instruments of contraction,[85]
gave us to enjoy the spirits of life,[86]
set firm within us the limbs of action,
nourished us with the good things of provision,
enriched us with His bounty
and contented us with his favors.[87]
Then He commanded us in order to test our obedience
and prohibited us in order to try our gratitude.[88]
So we deviated from the path of His command
and journeyed in the trackless wastes of His prohibitions.[89]

But He hastened us not to punishment[90]
and sped us not to His vengeance.
Nay, He was patient with us in His mercy, through kindness,
and He awaited our return in His tenderness, through clemency.

And praise belongs to God, who guided us to repentance,
which we never would have gained save through His bounty.
Were we to count as His bounty it alone,
our benefit[91] from Him would have been fair,
His goodness with us great
and His bounty toward us vast.
And such was not His wont with repentance in the case of those who went before us.[92]
Assuredly He lifted from us that which we have not the strength to bear[93]
and He charges us not save to our capacity.[94]
He imposes upon us only ease[95]
and has left none of us with an argument or excuse.[96]
So perished is he among us who perishes in spite of Him[97]
and felicitous is he among us who lets Him be his quest.

And praise belongs to God to the extent of all that He is praised by those of His angels nearest to Him,
His creatures noblest in His sight
and His praisers most pleasing to Him,
a praise which surpasses other praises as our Lord surpasses all of His creation.

Then to Him belongs praise in place of His every blessing upon us
and upon all of His servants, those gone and those remaining,
to the number of all things His knowledge encompasses,
and in place of every one of these blessings,
whose number will be doubled and redoubled
always and forever until the Day of Resurrection;
a praise whose confines have no limit,

whose number has no reckoning,
whose extremity is never reached
and whose term is never interrupted;[98]
a praise which may prove a way to reach His obedience and pardon,
a means to His good-pleasure,
a cause of His forgiveness,
a path to His Paradise,
a guard against His vengeance,
a sanctuary from His wrath,
an aid to obeying Him,
a barrier against disobeying Him
and a help toward carrying out our duties and obligations toward Him;
a praise which may give us the good fortune to be among His felicitous Friends,[99]
and by which we may enter the ranks of those martyred[100]
by the swords of His enemies.
Surely He is a protecting Friend, Praiseworthy.[101]

2. *Prayer for the Morning and Evening*

Praise belongs to God, who created the night and the day by His strength,
differentiated them by His power
and appointed for each of them a determined limit
and an extended term.[102]
He makes each of them enter into its companion
and makes its companion enter into it,[103]
as an ordainment from Him for His servants
in that which He feeds them
and with which He causes them to grow.
So He created for them the night
that they might repose in it
from toilsome movements
and fatiguing activities.[104]
He made it a garment that they might clothe themselves in His rest
and His sleep,[105]

that it might be for them refreshment
and strength,
and that they might attain in it pleasure
and passion.
And He created for them the day to see
that they might seek something of His bounty within it,[106]
gain access to His provision
and spread freely on His earth
searching for that wherein lies the attainment of the immediate things of this world
and the acquisition of the deferred things of the world to come.
With all of this He sets them aright,
tries their tidings,[107]
and observes how they are in the times (set apart) for obeying Him,
the stages of what He has obligated (upon them)
and the situations in which His laws apply,
"That He may reward those who do evil with that which they have done,
and reward those who do good with goodness" (LIII, 31).

O God, so to Thee belongs the praise for the sky which Thou splittest into dawn for us,[108]
the light of the day which Thou givest us to enjoy thereby,
the places for seeking sustenance Thou makest us to see
and the striking of maladies from which Thou protectest us therein.
We and all things, all together, enter upon the morning belonging to Thee
— the heaven and the earth,
what Thou hast scattered in each of them,[109]
whether at rest or in motion,
stationary or journeying,
what ascends into the air
and what is hidden beneath the ground.
We enter upon the morning in Thy grasp.

Thy dominion and power encompass us
and Thy will embraces us.
We conduct ourselves according to Thy command[110]
and we go about our business under Thy direction.
Nothing belongs to us of the matter except as Thou hast decreed,
and nothing of the good except as Thou hast given.
This is a fresh, new day,
and it is a ready witness over us.
If we do good, it will bid farewell to us in praise,
and if we do evil, it will part from us in blame.[111]

O God, bless Muhammad and his household,
provide us with the fair companionship of this day
and protect us from parting with it badly,
whether by committing an offence
or perpetrating a minor or major sin.[112]
Within it grant us abundant good deeds
and empty us of evil deeds.
Between its two extremes cause us to be filled with praise,
thanksgiving,
reward,
provision (for the world to come),
bounty
and good-doing.
O God, ease our burden on the Noble Writers,[113]
fill our pages with our good deeds,[114]
and abase us not before them with our evil deeds.
O God, in each of the hours of the day appoint for us
a portion of Thy servants,[115]
a share of thankfulness toward Thee
and a faithful witness from Thy angels.

O God, bless Muhammad and his household,
and safeguard us from before us
and behind us
and from our right hands
and our left hands
and from all directions,[116]
with a safeguarding that will protect against

disobedience to Thee,
guide unto Thy obedience
and engender Thy love.

O God, bless Muhammad and his household,
and give us success today and tonight and in all of our days
to work for good,
abandon evil,
give thanks for blessings,
follow traditions (*sunan*),
avoid innovation,
enjoin the right,
forbid the wrong,[117]
defend Islam,
diminish falsehood and abase it,
aid the truth and exalt it,
guide those who are astray,
help the weak
and extend a hand to the distressed.

O God, bless Muhammad and his household,
and make this day the most blessed day we have known,
the most excellent companion we have accompanied
and the best time we have passed.
Place us among the most satisfied of all Thy creatures whom night and day have passed by,
the most thankful for the blessings Thou has vouchsafed,
the firmest in the injunctions Thou hast promulgated
and the most scrupulous in what Thou hast warned against in Thy prohibitions.

O God, surely I call Thee to witness
— and Thou art sufficient witness —[118]
and I call to witness Thy heaven and Thy earth
and whomsoever Thou makest to dwell in them
of Thy angels and Thy other creatures,
on this day,
at this hour,
in this night
and within this my abode

that I testify that Thou art God,
there is no god but Thou,
upholding justice,[119]
equitable in judgment,
tender to servants,
Master of the dominion,[120]
merciful to creatures;
and that Muhammad is Thy servant and Thy messenger
and he whom Thou hast chosen from among Thy creatures.
Thou didst charge him with Thy message and he delivered it,[121]
Thou didst command him to counsel his community and he counselled it.
O God, so bless Muhammad and his household
the most Thou hast blessed any of Thy creatures.
Bestow upon him on our behalf the most excellent of what Thou hast given any of Thy servants,
and recompense him in our stead with the most excellent and generous recompense that Thou hast given any of Thy prophets on behalf of his community.
Truly Thou art All-gracious with immense blessings,
the Forgiver of great sins,
and Thou art more compassionate than every possessor of compassion.
So bless Muhammad and his household,
the virtuous, the pure,
the most excellent and noble.

C. Muhammad al-Mahdī, the Twelfth Imam

Prayer for the month of Rajab

Shaykh al-Ṭūsī has related that this noble writing came out of the Sacred Precinct on the hand of that great Shaykh, Abū Jaᶜfar Muḥammad ibn ᶜUthmān ibn Saᶜīd[122] *— may God be pleased with him. Recite it on each day of the month of Rajab.*

In the Name of God, the Merciful, the Compassionate
O God, I ask Thee by the meaning of all that by which Thou art called upon by those who govern with Thy authority:
those who are entrusted with Thy mystery,
welcome Thy command,
extol Thy power,
and proclaim Thy majesty.
I ask Thee by Thy will which speaks within them, for Thou hast appointed them
mines for Thy words,
and pillars of the profession of Thy Unity, Thy signs and Thy stations,
which are never interrupted in any place.
Through them knows he who knows Thee.
There is no difference between Thee and them,
save that they are Thy servants and Thy creation,
their doing and undoing is in Thy hand,
their origin is from Thee and their return is to Thee.
They are aides, witnesses, testers, defenders, protectors and searchers.
With them Thou filled Thy heaven and Thy earth until it became manifest that there is no god but Thou.
So I ask Thee by (all of) that,
and by the positions of Thy mercy's might
and by Thy Stations and Marks
that Thou bless Muhammad and His household
and increase me in faith and steadfastness.

O Inward in His outwardness and Outward in His inwardness and hiddenness!
O Separator of light and darkness!
O described by other than (His) Essence and well-known in other than (His) likeness!
Delimitator of every delimited thing!
Witness of all that is witnessed!
Bringer into existence of every existent!
Counter of everything counted!
Depriver of all that is deprived!

There is none worshipped but Thou,
Possessor of Grandeur and Generosity!
O He who is not conditioned by "how" or determined by "where"!
O veiled from every eye!
O Everlasting!
O eternally Self-subsistent and Knower of all that is known!
Bless Muhammad and his household
and Thy elect servants,
Thy mankind in veils,[123]
Thy angels brought nigh,
and the untold multitudes (of angels) set in ranks and encircling (the Throne).[124]
And bless us in this our venerated and honored month
and the sacred months that follow it.
In it bestow blessings upon us copiously,
make large our portions,
and fulfill for us (our) oaths,
by Thy most tremendous, most tremendous, greatest and noblest Name,
which Thou placed upon the day, and it brightened, and upon the night, and it darkened.
And forgive us that of ourselves which Thou knowest and we know not,
preserve us from sins with the best of preservations,
suffice us with the sufficiencies of Thy determination,
favor us with Thy fair regard,
leave us not to other than Thee,
hold us not back from Thy goodness,
bless us in the lifespans Thou hast written for us,
set aright for us the inmost center of our hearts,
give us protection from Thee,[125]
cause us to act with the fairest of faith,
and bring us to the month of fasting[126]
and the days and years that come after it,
O Lord of Majesty and Splendor!

NOTES

1 See C. Padwick, *Muslim Devotions*, London, 1961.

2 See *Shiʿite Islam*, pp. 210-11.

3 Cf. Quran LXXIII, 20: "And lend to God a good loan. Whatever good you shall forward to your soul's account, you shall find it with God as better, and mightier a wage."

4 Cf. Quran XL, 43. In another place, using a different root form for the verb "return", the Quran says in one of the verses most often heard in the Islamic world, "Surely we belong to God, and to Him we return" (II, 156).

5 Cf. Quran LXXVI, 1: "Has there come on man a while of time when he was a thing unremembered?"

6 The sin of breaking God's covenant is often described in the Quran. For example, "Such as break the covenant of God after its solemn binding . . . they shall be the losers." (II, 27). And "Crying lies to the messengers" is often mentioned as a major sin of past nations, e.g., "And the people of Noah, when they cried lies to the Messengers . . ." (XXV, 37).

7 Cf. Quran LXXV, 36-37: "What, does man reckon he shall be left to roam at will? Was he not a sperm-drop spilled? . . ."

8 Reference to Quran XXXIX, 6: "He created you in the wombs of your mothers, creation after creation, in a threefold gloom."

9 Cf. Quran XVIII, 52: "I made them not to witness the creation of the heavens and the earth, nor their own creation . . . ."

10 Cf. Quran XVI, 13: "And that which He has multiplied for you in the earth of diverse hues. Surely in that is a sign for a people who remember."

11 Reference to the Imam's descent from the Prophet. Cf. the first selection from ʿAlī above (p. 29).

12 Cf. Quran XIV, 7: "And when your Lord proclaimed: If you give thanks, I will give you more . . . ."

13 Cf. Quran XXX, 11: "God produces creation, then He reproduces it, then unto Him you will be returned." Also XXIX, 19; XXX, 27.

14 Cf. Quran XIV, 34 and XVI, 18: "And if you count God's blessing, you will never number it."

15 The "curtain of the heart" (*ḥijāb al-qalb*) is the pericardium.

16 The windpipe is not mentioned in some editions of *Mafātīḥ al-jinān*.

17 Cf. Quran XIX, 88-91: "And they say, 'The All-merciful has taken unto Himself a son.' You have indeed advanced something hideous! The heavens are wellnigh rent of it and the earth split asunder, and the mountains wellnigh fall

down crashing for that they have attributed to the All-merciful a son . . . ."

18 In the famous *ḥadīth* concerning *iḥsān* or "spiritual virtue" it is said that "Spiritual virtue is that you should worship God as if you were seeing him, and if you see Him not, He nonetheless sees thee."

19 Cf. Quran XLIII, 36: "Whoso blinds himself to the Remembrance of the All-merciful, to him We assign a Satan for comrade."

20 Cf. Quran LXIV, 3: "He shaped you and made good your shapes". See also XL, 64.

21 Cf. Quran XXVI, 79: " . . . who created me, and Himself guides me, and Himself gives me to eat and drink . . .".

22 Cf. Quran LIII, 48: "And that He it is Who enriches and contents."

23 Some editions add here the phrase "other than Thee".

24 Cf. Quran IX, 55: "So let not their possessions or their children please thee; God only desires thereby to chastise them in this present life, and that their souls should depart while they are unbelievers."

25 I.e., Mecca and the land surrounding it.

26 The "Sacred Monument", known as Muzdalifah, is the place where the pilgrims spend the night after the day at Arafat. Cf. Quran II, 198: "When you press on from Arafat, remember God by the Sacred Monument."

27 I.e., the Kaᶜbah, called the "Ancient House" in reference to the tradition that it was constructed by Abraham. See Quran XXII, 29 and 33; also XIV, 35-7.

28 Cf. Quran II, 125: "And when We made the House a resort for mankind and a sanctuary . . . ."

29 A further reference to the Prophet's blood descent from the Abrahamic line of prophets.

30 Israfil is the angel who according to Islamic tradition blows the trumpet at the time of the Resurrection.

31 The Criterion (*al-furqān*), is one of the names of the Quran, mentioned several times in its text, such as III, 4 and XXV, 1.

32 *Kāf Hā' Yā'Ayn Ṣād* are Arabic letters which appear at the beginning of the chapter of Maryam, Quran XIX. *Ṭā' Hā'* and *Yā' Sīn* are also letters appearing at the beginning of Quranic chapters, XX and XXXVI respectively, from which the chapters take their names. "The Wise Quran" is a title which appears in Quran XXXVI, 2.

33 *Al-Sattār*, "He who covers (faults and sins)", is one of the names of God.

34 Cf. Quran III, 13: "God confirms with His help whom He will."

35 Cf. Quran III, 160: "If God helps you, none can overcome you."

36 *Akram al-asmā'*. God's "fairest names" (*al-asmā' al-ḥusnā*) are referred to several times in the Quran, such as VII, 180 and XX, 8.

37 For the story of Joseph in the Quran see chapter XII.

38 Cf. Quran XXI, 83-84 and XXXVIII, 42-45.

39 Cf. Quran XXXVII, 102-105 and XIV, 39.

40 See Quran XXI, 89-90.

41 The story of Jonah and the "fish" is referred to in Quran LXVIII, 48-50.

42 Cf. Quran XXVI, 63-66 etc.

43 Cf. Quran XXV, 48: "And He it is Who sends the winds, glad tidings heralding His mercy, and We send down purifying water from the sky." See

also VII, 57 and XXX, 46.

44 Cf. Quran XVIII, 59: "Thy Lord is the Forgiver, Full of Mercy. If He took them to task (now) for what they earn, He would hasten on the doom for them; but theirs is an appointed term from which they will find no escape."

45 Reference to the story of Moses and the sorcerers, related several times in the Quran, especially VII, 111-126; XX, 62-73 and XXVI, 36-51.

46 A divine Name used in Quran XXX, 50 and XLI, 39.

47 Cf. Quran III, 26: "Thou exaltest whom Thou wilt, and Thou abasest whom Thou wilt."

48 Again reference to Quran XIV, 34 and XVI, 18.

49 Cf. Quran LIII, 48: "He it is who enriches and contents."

50 Cf. Quran XCIII, 6: "Did He not find thee an orphan and shelter Thee?"

51 Cf. Quran VII, 10: "We have established you in the earth . . .".

52 Cf. Quran VI, 150: "To God belongs the argument conclusive."

53 Cf. Quran XLI, 19-20: "Upon the day when God's enemies are mustered to the Fire duly disposed, till when they are come to it, their hearing, their eyes and their skins bear witness against them concerning what they have been doing."

54 Cf. Quran XXVII, 62: "He who answers the constrained, when he calls unto Him, and removes the evil and appoints you to be successors in the earth."

55 Cf. Quran XLI, 4 and XXXIII, 46.

56 Cf. Quran XXI, 107.

57 The symbolism of light and darkness is employed often in the Quran, not to mention its usage in Sufism and philosophy, such as the School of Illumination (*ishrāq*) of Suhrawardī. A good example of Quranic usage is the following: "God is the Protector of the believers; He brings them forth from the shadows into the light" (II, 257). There is also the famous "Light Verse" (XXIV, 35), which contains the sentence "God guides to His Light whom He will."

58 Cf. Quran XLII, 28.

59 Cf. Quran XVII, 30.

60 Again a reference to the rites performed on the Day of ᶜArafah. The "Sacred House" is of course the Kaᶜbah.

61 Cf. Quran LXV, 12.

62 The word "destroy" (*ahlak*, from whose root is derived the word "those who perish", *hālikūn*) is used repeatedly in the Quran in reference to God's punishment of the evildoers, expecially those of generations and ages past, as a sign and a warning for those present. For example, "Have they not regarded how We destroyed before them many a generation . . ." (VI, 6). See also X, 14; XIX, 98; XXI, 9; etc.

63 Cf. Quran II, 58: "We will forgive you your sins and will increase (reward) for the right-doers."

64 Cf. Quran IX, 104: "God is He who accepts repentance from His servants."

65 This sentence is almost a word for word quotation of Quran XVII, 44.

66 Cf. Quran CVI, 4: "Let them serve the Lord of this House who has . . . made them safe from fear."

67 Cf. Quran III, 54: "And they devised, and God devised, and God is the best of devisers." See also Quran XIII, 42; XXVII, 50, etc.

68 Cf. Quran VII, 182-183: "And those who cry lies to Our signs — step by

step We lead them on from whence they know not." See also LXVIII, 44.

69 Cf. Quran IV, 142: "The hypocrites seek to trick God, but God is tricking them."

70 A divine Name appearing in Quran VI, 62.

71 At this point the compiler remarks that some sources add another section to Imam Ḥusayn's prayer, a section which he then relates himself. Other authorities, such as Majlisī, express their doubts as to the authenticity of this last section. In fact it is almost certainly by Ibn ᶜAṭā'allāh al-Iskandarī, and therefore I have not translated it here. Readers interested will find a translation in V. Danner, *Ibn ᶜAṭā'illāh's Sufi Aphorisms*, Leiden, 1973, pp. 64-9. See W. Chittick, "A Shādhilī Presence in Shiᶜite Islam", *Sophia Perennis*, vol. I, no. 1, 1975, pp. 97-100.

72 In *Talkhīṣ al-riyāḍ*, a commentary on the *Ṣaḥīfah* (Tehran, 1381/1961-2, p. 34) al-Sayyid ᶜAlīkhān al-Shīrāzī (d. 1120/1708-9), mentions an objection that some people might be tempted to make here, i.e., that "the pronoun 'them' refers to all creatures, while certain of the creatures are God's enemies, so how should this statement be correct? The answer is that in its essential and primordial nature according to which it was originally created (cf. Quran XXX, 30), every soul loves and seeks the good, and all good flows from God's goodness, just as all existence flows from His Being. Therefore in reality the creatures love only Him, even if their love be in accordance with His Name 'the Outward' and in terms of external beauty and goodness, or worldly station and property, or anything else." Then al-Shīrāzī quotes Ibn al-ᶜArabī in the *Futūḥāt al-makkiyyah:* "None loves any but his Creator, but He is hidden from him under the veil of Zaynab, Suᶜād, Hind and Laylā (names of women), dirhams and dinars, worldly position, and all that exists in the world, for one of the causes of love is beauty — which belongs only to Him — since beauty incites love through its very nature. Now, 'God is beautiful, and He loves beauty' (a saying of the Prophet), and thus He loves Himself. Another cause of love is virtue (*iḥsān*), and virtue is only perfect when it comes from God: None is virtuous but God (*lā muḥsin illa-llāh*). So if you love beauty, you love none other than God, for He is the Beautiful; and if you love virtue, you love none other than He, for He is the Virtuous. In every case, the object of love is none other than God." This is one of the themes of the *Lamaᶜāt* of Fakhr al-Dīn ᶜIrāqī, translated by W. C. Chittick and P. L. Wilson, New York, forthcoming.

73 Cf. Quran LXXXIX, 15-16: "As for man, whenever his Lord tries him, and honours him, and blesses him, then he says, 'My Lord has honoured me'."

74 On the meaning of "clear text of His Book", see above, p. 56, note 48.

75 Literally, "concerning His affair (*amr*)". Al-Shīrāzī explains "His affair" as meaning "either the knowledge of His nature and attributes, or of His religion and *Sharīᶜah*" (p. 56).

76 Here the Interval or "isthmus" (*barzakh*) refers to the time between death and resurrection. It is referred to in Quran XXIII, 100: "And beyond them is an Interval until the day when they are raised." See *Shiᶜite Islam*, pp. 164-5; also the *Encyclopedia of Islam* (new edition), vol. 1, pp. 1071-2.

77 According to a *ḥadīth* of the Prophet, "Verily the passage from the grave to the Plain of Gathering (*ᶜarṣat al-maḥshar*) on the Day of Resurrection will be burdensome for some people and smooth for others" (quoted by al-Shīrāzī, p. 62).

78 The Stations of the Witnesses (*mawāqif al-ashhād*) are the stations of angels, prophets, Imams and believers who at the Resurrection act as witnesses over the deeds performed by men during their earthly lives. These Witnesses are referred to in Quran XI, 18 and XL, 51.

79 ᶜIlliyūn, mentioned in Quran LXXXIII, 18 and 19, is variously interpreted. For example, it is said to be the highest level of heaven, or a place in the seventh heaven where the souls of believers are taken after their death, or the book in the seventh heaven in which are written the deeds of angels and of righteous men and jinn.

80 Cf. Quran LXXV, 7 ff.: "But when sight is confounded and the moon is eclipsed and sun and moon are united, on that day man will cry: Whither to flee!"

81 Cf. Quran III, 106: "The day when some faces are blackened, and some faces whitened. As for those whose faces are blackened — 'Did you disbelieve after you had believed? Then taste the chastisement for that you disbelieved.' "

82 Cf. Quran XL, 64: "And He shaped you, and shaped you well, and provided you with the good things."

83 Besides the many Quranic verses which point to man's "central" position in the Universe because of his capacity as viceregent or caliph of God, the being who partakes of all of the divine Names and Attributes, there are many other verses indicating one of the major results of his special rank: his domination over all of the Universe. For example: "And He subjected to you the night and day, and the sun and moon" (XVI, 12); "Have you not seen how God has subjected to you whatsoever is in the heavens and the earth?" (XXXI, 20). See also XIV, 32-33; XXII, 65, etc.

84 The Arabic reads "*lā matā*", which according to al-Shirāzī can be interpreted in two ways: either it means "Nay (it is impossible to thank Him), when (could it be possible?)", or "(It is) not (correct to say) when, (for that implies that it is possible to thank Him)" (p. 75).

85 According to al-Shirāzī, the reference is to the expansion and contraction of the organs of the body, such as nerves, muscles, veins, arteries, flesh, etc. (p. 75).

86 Or "breaths of life". Al-Shirāzī comments: "*Arwāḥ* may be the plural of *rūḥ*, meaning spirit, in which case the meaning is explained by the tradition transmitted from Imams ᶜAlī, al-Bāqir and al-Ṣādiq: 'There are five (spirits) possessed by Those Brought Nigh (cf. Quran LVI, 11): the spirit of sanctity, through which they know all things; the spirit of faith, through which they worship God; the spirit of power, through which they wage holy war against enemies and attend to their livelihood; the spirit of passion, through which they partake in the joy of food and marriage; and the spirit of the body, through which they move and advance. There are four spirits possessed by the Companions of the Right (Quran LVI, 8), since they lack the spirit of sanctity; and there are three possessed by the Companions of the Left (Quran LVI, 8) and beasts, since they lack (the spirit of sanctity and) the spirit of faith.

"*Arwāḥ* may also be the plural of *rawḥ*, which is a 'breath of wind'. The arteries of the body possess two movements, contractive and expansive. It is their function to draw 'smoky' vapors from the heart with their contractive movement and to attract with their expansive movement fresh and pure breaths of air, through which the heart is refreshed and its natural heat is drawn from it. By means of this 'breath of wind' the animal faculty and the natural heat are diffused throughout the body. Thus this breath of wind by which the heart refreshes itself is the 'breath of life'. If it is cut off from the heart for a period of time, life also will be cut off from it" (p. 75).

87 Cf. Quran LIII, 48: "And that He it is who enriches and contents."

88 Al-Shīrāzī quotes here a tradition of Imam Ja^cfar al-Ṣādiq: "Gratitude for blessings is to avoid what is forbidden" (p. 77).

89 Al-Shīrāzī explains that "path" is used in the singular and "trackless wastes" in the plural because the "straight path" is one, while the ways of going astray are many: "This is My straight path, so follow it. Follow not other ways, lest ye be parted from His way" (Quran VI, 154).

90 Cf. Quran X, 12: "If God should hasten unto men evil (i.e., punishment), as they would hasten good, their term would be already decided for them."

91 *Balā'*, translated here as "benefit", usually means "test", "trial", or "misfortune", but here it is used as in Quran VIII, 17, which Arberry, following the commentators, translates, " . . . that He might confer on the believers a fair benefit." See al-Shīrāzī, p. 81.

92 According to Al-Shīrāzī (p. 81), this is a reference to the difference between God's "wont" (*sunnah*) concerning repentance with the Muslims and His wont with the Jews. From the former He only asks regret (*al-nadam*), but from the latter in addition to regret He also asks "killing of themselves" (*qatl anfusihim*) as indicated in Quran II, 54: "And when Moses said unto his people: O my people! Ye have wronged yourselves by your choosing of the calf (for worship) so turn in repentance to your Creator; and kill yourselves."

93 Cf. Quran II, 286: "Our Lord! Lay not on us such a burden as Thou didst lay on those before us! Our Lord! Impose not on us that which we have not the strength to bear!"

94 Cf. Quran II, 286: "God charges no soul save to its capacity." According to al-Shīrāzī this sentence is a reference to the obligations which — according to Muslim beliefs — God imposed upon the Jews, such as, "the performance of fifty canonical prayers per day, the payment of one-fourth of their property in alms . . . ." Also it is a reference to the verse, "For the evildoing of those of Jewry, We have forbidden them certain good things that were permitted to them" (Quran IV, 160). See al-Shīrāzī, pp. 82-83.

95 Cf. such Quranic verses as, "He has chosen you and has not laid upon you in religion any hardship" (XXII, 78).

96 Cf. Quran IV, 165: "Messengers of good cheer and warning, in order that mankind might have no argument against God after the messengers"; and LXVI, 7: "O ye who disbelieve! Make no excuses for yourselves this day. Ye are only being paid for what ye used to do."

97 "In spite of Him" (*^calayh*) is explained by al-Shīrāzī as meaning, "In spite of God's disliking (that he should perish), for He is not pleased that any of His servants should perish. Thus it is that He spreads His mercy over them and hurries them not to punishment for their sins. Rather He is patient with them in His mercy and waits for their return in His kindness. He opens for them the door of repentance, lifts from them that which they have not the strength to bear and charges them only to their capacity. So it is as if whoever

perishes because of his evil deeds after all of this does so in spite of the fact that God does not want him to do so" (p. 84).

98 Al-Shīrāzī points out that the Imam first gives the Day of Resurrection as the outer limit of His praise, then as a sort of admonition lest he be misunderstood extends it in conformity with Him who is praised. In the same way in another prayer he says, "A praise eternal (*khālid*) with Thy Eternity" (p. 88).

99 The term "friend" (*walī*) of God, referred to for example in the verse, "He befriends the righteous" (VIII, 190), is interpreted in many ways. According to certain theologians the *walī* is a person whose belief is sound, who performs his religious duties and who as a result has attained proximity to God. In Sufism the term takes on a technical meaning and is often translated as "saint". See al-Shīrāzī, pp. 91-92.

100 According to a *ḥadīth* of the Prophet related through the sixth Imam, "Beyond every one who possesses piety, there are other pious acts, until he is killed in the path of God: when he has been killed in the path of God, there is no further act of piety" (al-Shīrāzī, p. 93). See also such Quranic verses as III, 157; III, 169 and IV, 74.

101 Al-Shīrāzī remarks, "The appropriateness of terminating this prayer, which is dedicated to praise, with the name 'Praiseworthy' is obvious" (p. 93).

102 Cf. Quran XXXVI, 39: "It is not for the sun to overtake the moon, nor does the night outstrip the day."

103 Cf. Quran XXXV, 13: "He makes the night enter into the day and He makes the day enter into the night." The same or similar verses occur several times in the Quran, including III, 27; XXII, 61; XXXI, 29; and LVII, 6.

104 Reference to Quran X, 68 and several identical or similar verses: "It is He who made for you the night to repose in it."

105 Cf. Quran XXV, 47: "It is He who appointed the night for you to be a garment and sleep for a rest . . ." and other similar verses.

106 Cf. Quran XVII, 12: "We . . . made the sign of the day to see, and that you may seek bounty from your Lord" and other similar verses.

107 Cf. Quran XLVII, 31: "And We shall assuredly try you until We know those of you who struggle and are steadfast, and try your tidings."

108 Cf. Quran VI, 97: "He splits the sky into dawn . . ."

109 Cf. Quran XLV, 3-4: "Surely in the heavens and the earth there are signs for the believers; and in your creation, and the crawling things He scatters abroad, there are signs for a people having sure faith."

110 Al-Shīrāzī points out that "command" (*amr*) here means the "ontological (*takwīnī*) command" (p. 217). Philosophers and theologians distinguish this, which refers to the laws of creation and which all must obey by the very nature of things, from the "legislative (*tashrīʿī*) command", which refers to the laws set down by God in revelation and which man can obey or disobey according to his own free will. The "ontological command" is referred to in such verses as: "His command, when He desires a thing, is to say to it 'Be', and it is" (XXXVI, 81).

111 Al-Shīrāzī quotes a tradition from the sixth Imam: "No day comes upon the son of Adam without saying to him, 'O son of Adam, I am a new day and I am a witness against thee. So speak good in me and work good in me, and I shall witness for thee upon the Day of Resurrection, for after this thou shalt never

see me again' " (p. 218).

112 The distinction between minor (*ṣaghīrah*) and major (*kabīrah*) sins is much discussed in Islamic theology. For a sample of Shi[c]ite views, see al-Shīrāzī, pp. 219-223.

113 The angels who write down the deeds of men are referred to in Quran LXXXII, 10-11: "Yet there are over you watchers noble, writers who know whatever you do." In explaining what is meant by "Ease our burdens on them", al-Shīrāzī quotes the celebrated Safavid theologian, Shaykh-i Bahā'ī: "This is an allusion to seeking protection with God from excessive talk and from excessive occupation with what entails neither worldly nor other-worldly gain: then the Noble Writers will have fewer of our words and deeds to record." The Prophet said, "I am astonished at the son of Adam: his two angels are on his shoulders, his speech is their pen and his saliva their ink. How can he speak of that which does not concern him?" (p. 224).

114 Cf. Quran LXXXI, especially 10-14: "And when the pages are laid open, and when the sky is torn away, and when hell is ignited, and when the garden is brought nigh, (then) every soul will know what it has made ready."

115 According to al-Shīrāzī the meaning is, "Appoint for us some of Thy servants that we may seek illumination through their lights and follow in their tracks." He adds a long discussion of the elevated position of the "servant" (*[c]abd*), noting that in his highest form he is even more exalted than the messenger. This is the reason for the word order of the formula which every Muslim repeats in his canonical prayers: "Muhammad is His servant and His messenger". Al-Shīrāzī also points out that some manuscripts read "servanthood" (*[c]ibādah*) for "servants" (*[c]ibād*) and that this is more in keeping with the context (pp. 227-8).

116 This is a reference to the words of Satan in the Quran: "Then I shall come on them from before them and from behind them and from their right hands and their left hands; Thou wilt not find most of them thankful" (VII, 17).

117 *Al-amr bi-l-ma[c]rūf wa-l-nahy [c]an al-munkar*, according to Shi[c]ites one of the pillars of Islam, and a command which is repeated many times in the Quran, such as VII, 157, and IX, 71.

118 The verse "God is sufficient witness" occurs several times in the Quran, such as IV, 79; X, 29, etc.

119 These two lines are an almost word for word quotation from Quran III, 18.

120 A divine Name occurring in Quran III, 26.

121 Cf. such verses as the following: "Say: 'Obey God and obey the Messenger; then if you turn away, only upon him rests what is laid on him .... It is only for the Messenger to deliver the Message" (XXIV, 34).

122 The second of the Twelfth Imam's four deputies, referred to in the introduction to Part III, p. 92.

123 I.e., "normal" men, who are veiled from and ignorant of God's true nature.

124 *Al-Ṣāffīn*, the angels "who set the ranks", are referred to in Quran XXXVII, 165; and *al-ḥāffīn* are referred to in XXXIX, 75: "And thou shalt see the angels encircling about the Throne proclaiming the praise of their Lord."

125 This recalls the Prophet's supplication: "I seek refuge in Thy forgiveness from Thy punishment, I seek refuge in Thy approval from Thy anger, I seek

refuge in Thee from Thee!"

126 In the Islamic calendar Rajab is followed by Sha^cbān and then the month of fasting, or Ramaḍān, which is considered to the holiest and most blessed month of the year.

Appendix

The Twelve Imams[1]

The word "*imām*" in Arabic means "leader". In Islamic terminology it generally refers to any person who leads others in prayer. According to the early Sunni theologians, *the* Imam is the leader of the Islamic community, and his function is to enforce the revealed Law or Sharīᶜah. As such the term is equivalent to "caliph". In Sunnism it may also be an honorific term, given to certain important religious leaders, such as Imam Shāfiᶜī, founder of one of the four Sunni schools of law. In Twelve-Imam Shi'ism it has two important meanings. As in Sunnism, the leader of others in prayer is called an "imam", especially the person who performs this function on a regular basis in a mosque. But more specifically, an Imam is one of the twelve successors of the Prophet listed below.

The specific meaning given to the word "Imam" in Shi'ism can not be understood until one grasps the basic difference between the Sunni and Shi'ite branches of Islam. The roots of this difference are to be found in the differing views held by the companions of the Prophet concerning the nature of his successor or caliph. The Prophet himself performed three basic functions: He acted as the means whereby a celestial book, the Quran, was revealed by God to mankind. Thus he was the founder of a world religion. He was also the ruler of the early Islamic community, which means that he enforced the Sharīᶜah which God had revealed through the Quran. Finally he was the possessor of spiritual illumination and vision, and as such he could interpret the inner meaning of the Revelation and guide men upon the ascending stages of the path of spiritual perfection.

According to the majority of Muslims, the Sunnis, the successor of the Prophet must fulfill only one of these functions, i.e., he should enforce the Sharīʿah. Muhammad had been the last Prophet, so there could be no prophet after him. And there was no way the community could guarantee that his successors would possess spiritual vision and illumination, for like prophecy, these things are divinely bestowed (although unlike prophecy, they could still be possessed by men). But undoubtedly, the Prophet's successor could act as a ruler and enforce the Sharīʿah. In fact, the earthly existence of Islam largely depended upon this function being fulfilled, particularly at its beginning. Finally, the Sunnis held that the Prophet had not appointed a successor during his lifetime, so it was up to them to choose one.

But the minority group, known as the "Shi'ites" (the "partisans" of ʿAlī), maintained that the Prophet's successor must not only enforce the Sharīʿah, he must also possess divinely illuminated wisdom and be the spiritual guide of men. Since this latter function is bestowed by God and cannot be judged by the majority of men, the Prophet's successor must be divinely appointed, as expressed in the Prophet's wishes. And the Shi'ites hold that the Prophet had in fact appointed ʿAlī as his caliph.[2]

This difference in view between the Shi'ites and Sunnis was often expressed in political terms, resulting in a good deal of strife in the early centuries of Islam between certain Shi'ite groups and the Umayyad and Abbasid caliphs. For, as far as the Shi'ites were concerned, the Imams were the only completely legitimate successors to the Prophet. The first, ʿAlī, was appointed by the Prophet himself, and each in turn was appointed by his predecessor according to divine decree.

Fāṭimah

The beloved daughter of the Prophet from Khadījah, Fāṭimah was born in Mecca five years before the beginning of the Prophet's mission. She was so loved by the Prophet that he called her "a part of me." In 2/624 she married ʿAlī ibn Abī Ṭālib from whom she bore three sons, Ḥasan, Ḥusayn and Muḥsin (who died stillborn), and two daughters, Zaynab and Umm Kulthūm. She was at the Prophet's bedside at the moment of his death and fought for her husband's succession to the caliphate. She died six months after her father in the year 11/633 and is buried in the Baqī^{c} cemetery in Medina. It is said that when she was born the whole sky became illuminated; therefore she is called al-Zahrā', the "Radiant." She is the mother of the Shi'ite Imams and is considered the most holy of Muslim women.

The Imams

I. The First Imam, ^{c}Alī (b. A.D. 600, d. A.H. 40/A.D. 661)

He was the son of the Prophet's paternal uncle, Abū Ṭālib, who had raised the Prophet like his own son and protected him after he declared his mission. According to the Shi'ites, ^{c}Alī was the first to accept the new religion at the hands of the Prophet, at the age of ten. He was the greatest warrior of early Islam, and according to his partisans was appointed by the Prophet as his successor at a place known as "Ghadīr al-Khumm". He became the fourth Sunni caliph, the last of the "Rightly-Guided Caliphs", after the death of ^{c}Uthmān. He was finally assassinated by followers of the Khawārij (an early schismatic sect), after five years as caliph. He is buried in Najaf in Iraq.

II. The Second Imam, al-Ḥasan (3/62 -50/670)

He was the elder son of ^{c}Alī by the Prophet's daughter Fāṭimah. He laid claim to the caliphate for some six months after the death of his father, but was finally forced to surrender it to Mu^{c}āwiyah. For the rest of his life he lived in Medina in seclusion. He is buried in the Baqī^{c} cemetery in Medina.

III. The Third Imam, al-Ḥusayn (4/62 -61/680)

The younger son of ^{c}Alī by Fāṭimah, like his brother he lived most of his life quietly in Medina under the watchful eyes of the caliph's officials and spies. When Mu^{c}āwiyah's son Yazīd became caliph, he demanded allegiance from al-Ḥusayn, who refused to give it. Finally al-Ḥusayn felt it necessary to go into battle against Yazīd to protest against the injustices which were being carried out in the name of Islam. He and a small group of followers including most of his immediate family were cruelly massacred at Karbala. The day of his martyrdom ("^{c}Āshūrā") has become the most solemn day of the Shi'ite calendar, marked by processions and universal mourning. Its celebration symbolizes the whole ethos of Shi'ism. He is buried in Karbala in Iraq.

IV. The Fourth Imam, ^{c}Alī, known as Zayn al-^{c}Ābidīn and al-Sajjād (38/658- 95/712)

The son of Imam al-Ḥusayn by the daughter of Yazdigird, the last Sassanid king of Iran, he was not able to carry arms at Karbala because of illness, and thus he was saved the fate of his three brothers. For most of his life he lived in seclusion in Medina, having contact with only a few select followers. His piety — which is reflected in his collected prayers, *al-Ṣaḥīfat al-sajjādiyyah* — is proverbial. He is buried in the Baqī^{c} cemetery in Medina.

V. The Fifth Imam, Muḥammad, known as al-Bāqir (57/675-114/732)

The son of the fourth Imam, he was present at Karbala at a young age. Because of changing political and religious conditions, among them the general revulsion following the events at Karbala, many people came to Medina to learn the religious and spiritual sciences from him. He trained numerous well-known men of religion, and mainly for this reason is the first Imam after ^{c}Alī from whom large numbers of traditions are recorded. He is buried in the Baqī^{c} cemetery in Medina.

VI. The Sixth Imam, Ja^{c}far, known as al-Ṣādiq (83/702-148/765)

The son of the fifth Imam, he lived in an increasingly favorable climate and was able to teach openly in Medina. Large numbers of scholars gathered around him to learn, including such famous Sunni figures as Abū Ḥanīfah, the founder of one of the four Sunni schools of law. Towards the end of Imam Ja^{c}far's life severe restrictions were placed upon his activities, as a result of growing Shi'ite unrest. More traditions are recorded from him than from all the other Imams together. He is so important for Twelve-Imam Shi'ite law that it is named the "Ja^{c}farī School" after him. He is buried in the Baqī' cemetery in Medina.

VII. The Seventh Imam, Mūsā, entitled al-Kāẓim (128/744-183/799)

The son of the sixth Imam, he was contemporary with such Abbasid caliphs as al-Manṣūr and Hārūn al-Rashīd. He lived most of his life in Medina with severe restrictions placed upon him and finally died in prison in Baghdad. After him, the Imams were often not able to live in their traditional home of Medina, but were forced to remain near the caliph in Baghdad or Samarra. He is buried in Kazimayn in Iraq.

VIII. The Eighth Imam, ^{c}Alī, known as al-Riḍā (148/765-

203/817)

The son of the seventh Imam, he lived in a period when the Abbasids were faced with increasing difficulties because of Shi'ite revolts. Finally the caliph al-Ma'mūn thought he would solve the problem by naming the Imam as his own successor, hoping thus to ensnare him in worldly affairs and turn the devotion of his followers away from him. After finally being able to persuade al-Riḍā to accept, al-Ma'mūn realized his mistake, for Shi'ism began to spread even more rapidly. Finally he is said to have had the Imam poisoned. Al-Riḍā is buried in Mashhad in Iran.

IX. The Ninth Imam, Muḥammad, known as al-Taqī (195/809-220/835)

The son of the eighth Imam, he was given the daughter of the caliph al-Ma'mūn in marriage and for a time was kept by the caliph in Baghdad. But he was able to return to Medina until the end of al-Ma'mūn's reign. The new caliph, al-Muᶜtaṣim, summoned him back to Baghdad where he died. He is buried in Kazimayn in Iraq.

X. The Tenth Imam, ᶜAlī, known as al-Naqī (212/827-254/868)

The son of the ninth Imam, he remained in Medina teaching the religious sciences until 243/857, when he was summoned to Samarra by the caliph al-Mutawakkil. There he was treated harshly by the caliph and his successors until he died. He is buried in Samarra.

XI. The Eleventh Imam, al-Ḥasan, called al-ᶜAskarī (232/845-260/872)

The son of the tenth Imam, he lived in close confinement in Samarra under the watchful eye of the caliph, especially since it was known that the Shi'ites were awaiting his son, the twelfth Imam, who was to be the promised Mahdī or "guided one", destined to remove injustice from the world. The eleventh Imam married the daughter of the Byzantine emperor, Nargis Khātūn, who, following instructions given her in a dream, had sold herself into slavery to become his wife. He is buried in Samarra.

XII. The Twelfth Imam, Muḥammad, known as al-Mahdī (b. 256/868)

The twelfth Imam lived in hiding under the protection and tutelage of his father until the latter's death. Then he went into "occultation". In other words, he became hidden from the eyes of ordinary men and appeared only to his Deputies (see p. 92.)

In the year 329/939 his "greater occultation" began. It will continue as long as God wills, but when he does appear once again, he will erase evil and injustice from the world.

NOTES

1 For a detailed account, see *Shi'ite Islam.*

2 For a profound and illuminating explanation of the basic difference in perspective represented by Sunnism and Shi'ism see F. Schuon, *Islam and the Perennial Philosophy*, London, 1976, ch. 5.

BIBLIOGRAPHY

The Sources of the Selections

Part I: From Muḥammad Bāqir Majlisī, *Biḥār al-anwār*, 110 vols., Tehran, 1380/1960-1 — 1390/1970-1.

A. The Prophet
1. Profession of Faith: vol. 4, pp. 287-8.
2. God's Attributes: vol. 3, pp. 303-4.

B. ᶜAlī
1. The Transcendent Lord: vol. 4, pp. 221-3.
2. *Via negativa:* vol. 4, pp. 247-8.
3. Firm Rooting in Knowledge: vol. 4, pp. 274-8.
4. The Fairest of Creators: vol. 4, pp. 313-5.
5. Oneness: vol. 3, pp. 206-7.
6. Discernment: vol. 4, p. 253.
7. The Vision of the Heart: vol. 4, pp. 304-6.

C. al-Bāqir: The Incomparable Lord: vol. 4, pp. 299-300.

D. Jaᶜfar
1. Seeing God: vol. 4, pp. 44-5.
2. The name that can be named . . .: vol. 4, pp. 160-1.

E. Mūsā: The Mighty and Majestic: vol. 4, p. 298.

F. ᶜAlī al-Riḍā
1. Profession of Unity: vol. 4, pp. 228-30.
2. The Veil: vol. 3, pp. 36-8.

Part II: From *Nahj al-balāghah*, ed. by Muḥyī al-Dīn Muḥammad ᶜAbd al-Ḥamīd, with the commentary of Muḥammad ᶜAbduh, 3 parts, Cairo, n.d., part 3, pp. 92-122.

Part III: The Spiritual Life

A. al-Ḥusayn, Prayer for the Day of ᶜArafah: From ᶜAbbās Qummī, *Mafātīḥ al-jinān*, Muḥammad Ḥasan ᶜIlmī edition, Tehran, 1381/1961, pp. 531-53; also Islāmiyyah edition, ed. by Muḥammad Bāqir Kamaraī', Tehran, 1379/1959-60, pp. 350-65.

B. ᶜAlī Zayn al-ᶜĀbidīn: the first and sixth prayers from *al-Ṣaḥīfat al-sajjādiyyah* (*Ṣaḥīfa-yi kāmila-yi sajjādiyyah*); with Persian translation by M. A. Shaᶜrānī, Islāmiyyah edition, Tehran, n.d., pp. 15-20, 32-6; with Persian translation by A. Fayḍ al-Islām, Tehran, 1375/1955-6, pp. 28-41, 68-75; with Persian translation by J. Fāḍil, Tehran, 1348/1969, pp. 47-50, 93-5.

C. The Twelfth Imam: Prayer for the Month of Rajab: *Mafātiḥ al-jinān*, pp. 279-81/184-6.

Other sources

ᶜAbduh, Muḥammad, *Sharḥ nahj al-balāghah*, printed with the edition of the *Nahj al-balāghah* mentioned in the sources of the selections above (Part II).

al-Fakīkī, T., *al-Rāᶜī wa-l-raᶜiyyah*, Najaf, 1940.

al-Hāshimī, Mīrzā Ḥabīballāh, *Minhāj al-barāᶜah fī sharḥ nahj al-balāghah*, vol. 20, Tehran, 1389/1969-70.

Ibn Abi-l-Ḥadīd, *Sharḥ nahj al-balāghah*, Beirut.

Ibn Maytham, *Sharḥ nahj al-balāghah*, Tehran lithographed edition, 1276/1859-60.

al-Kulaynī, *al-Usūl min al-kāfī*, ed. by Muḥammad Bāqir Kamara'ī, Tehran, 1388/1968-9.

al-Ṣadūq, *al-Tawḥīd*, ed. by Hāshim al-Ḥusaynī al-Ṭahrānī, Tehran, 1387/1967-8.

al-Shīrāzī, al-Sayyid ᶜAlīkhān, *Talkhīṣ al-riyāḍ*, vol. 1, Tehran, 1381/1961-2.

INDEX

mawṣūf, 30, 42, 43, 45.
Mecca, 92, 126, 136.
Medina, 137-9.
Mensing, J. P., 12.
merchants, 72, 76, 86.
Messenger (Muḥammad), 73, 77, 78, 87, 109, 110, 132.
Michael, 37, 101.
miqdār, 32.
miʿrāj, 54.
Mīr Dāmād, 10.
Mishkāt al-maṣābīḥ, 20.
mithāl, 25, 32, 33, 43.
Morgan, Kenneth, 10.
Moses, 37, 54, 127, 130.
mu'allif, 39.
Muʿāwiyah, 67, 137.
mubā'in, 27, 46, 47.
mubāsharah, 39.
mubāyanah, 45.
mudabbir, 46.
muḍāddah, 39.
mudānāh, 39.
mudh, 47, 63.
mudrik, 46.
mufarriq, 39, 74.
al-mughayyā', 42.
Muḥammad (Prophet), 26, 27, 29, 48, 67, 98, 100, 101, 108-10, 113, 120-4, 132.
Muḥammad al-Bāqir (the Fifth Imam), 9, 24, 40, 62, 129, 138.
Muḥammad al-Mahdī (the Twelfth Imam), 5, 6, 92, 122, 132, 139.
Muḥammad al-Taqī (the Ninth Imam), 139.
Muhammadan Light, 6, 55.
Muḥammad ibn ʿAbdallāh al-Khurāsānī, 48.
Muḥammad ibn Abī Bakr, 68.
Muhammadi Trust, 10, 11, 19.
Muḥarram, 92.
muḥkam, 56.
Muḥsin, 136.
muḥtasib, 79.
mujarrad, 53.
mukābadah, 56.
mukāyadah, 56.
mulḥidūn, 42.
Mullā Ṣadrā (Ṣadr al-Dīn Shīrāzī), 10, 12.
mumkināt, 60.
munshī', 49.
muqaddir, 39, 49.
muqāranah, 30, 39.
murīd, 39.
murū'ah, 86.
Mūsā (the Seventh Imam), 9, 24, 43, 55, 59, 138, 139.
mushabbihūn, 42.
mushrik(ūn), 43, 80.
Muslim (the author), 12, 15, 20.
Muslim(s), 5, 15, 25, 52, 67, 70, 72, 80, 84, 87, 91, 92, 136; *al-muslimīn*, 110.
mustawḥish, 41.
mutaghayyir, 65.
mutajallin, 39.
mutamakkināt, 53.
mutamāzij, 39.
mutashābih, 56.
mutawaḥḥid, 30.
mutawahhimīn, 32.
al-Mutawakkil, 139.
muzāyalah, 30, 46.
Muzdalifah, 126.

nadam, 130.
nafs, 30, 80.
nafy, 48; *nafy al-ṣifāt*, 30.
Nahj al-balāghah, 8, 9, 16-8, 54, 57, 59, 64, 67, 68.
nā'ib, 92.
Najaf, 137.
Nargis Khātūn, 139.
Nasr, S. H., 12, 13, 17, 19, 54, 60.
Naʿthal, 26, 27.
naʿt mawjūd, 30.
nihāyah, 60.
Ninth Imam (Muḥammad al-Taqī), 139.
niẓām, 45.
Noah, 125.
Noble Writers, 120.
al-nūr al-muḥammadī, 6.
nuṭq, 43.